Innovative Instruction: A Menu of Teaching Tools for Effective Student Learning

Innovative Instruction: A Menu of Teaching Tools for Effective Student Learning

by

Betty Shoemaker

Larry Lewin

Christopher-Gordon Publishers, Inc.
Norwood, Massachusetts

Copyright Acknowledgments

Every effort has been made to contact copyright holders for permission to reproduce borrowed material where necessary. We apologize for any oversights and would be happy to rectify them in future printings.

Figure 2.7, *CSR Learning Log* reprinted with permission from Janette Klingner.

Figure 2.14, *Shiloh Work Plan* reprinted with permission from M. J. Goeway.

Figure 2.15, *Fourth Year Spanish Class Calendar Work Plan* reprinted with permission from Franzi Thompson.

Figure 2.17, *Three Types of Questions* and Figure 2.18, *QAR Strategies*, from Raphael & Au (2003), Super QAR for Testwise Students. Chicago, IL: Wright Group/McGraw Hill. Reprinted with permission.

Figure 5.1, *Mexico Post Cards Directions* and Figure 5.26, *Invention Rubric* reprinted with permission from Terry Osgerby.

Figure 5.2, *Letters from Guatemala* and 5.13, *Monitoring Checklist for Historical Fiction* reprinted with permission from Lee Burton.

Figure 5.5, *Elements of Fiction Brochure Template* reprinted with permission from Coni Honn and Victoria Lamkey.

Figure 5.6, *Rainforest Brochure* reprinted with permission from Sue Walters.

Figure 5.10, *Sixth Grade Language Arts Technical Training Manual* reprinted with permission from Joanne Wesener.

Figure 5.16, *Monsters Before and After* activity reprinted with permission from Tracy Dabbs.

Figure 5.19, *High School Student's Supreme Court EGO* reprinted with permission from Vicky Ayers.

Figure 5.23, *Speech Checklist* reprinted with permission from Eddie Willig.

Chapter Seven interview conducted by Kay Mehas reprinted with permission.

Description of the *Unit Organizer Routine* included with permission from B. Keith Lenz.

Material from Eugene School District 4J, including *Key Words for Developing Focus Questions*, *Art Composition Scoring Guide*, *Writing Scoring Guide*, *Questioning Prompts Bookmarks*, and *District Norms for Oral Reading Fluency*, reprinted with permission.

Student work reprinted with permission.

Copyright © 2004 by Christopher-Gordon Publishers, Inc.

All rights reserved. Except for review purposes, no part of this material protected by this copyright notice may be reproduced or utilized in any form or by any means, electronic or mechanical, including photocopying, recording, or in any information and retrieval system, without the express written permission of the publisher or copyright holder.

Christopher~Gordon Publishers, Inc.
Bridging Theory and Practice

1502 Providence Highway, Suite #12
Norwood, Massachusetts 02062
800-934-8322
781-762-5577

Printed in the United States of America
10 9 8 7 6 5 4 3 2 1   07 06 05 04

ISBN: 1-929024-73-8
Library of Congress Catalogue Number: 2003113425

Dedication

Betty's Dedication

I dedicate this work to John Stacey, Robin Best, John Bezelj, Martha Harris, Janice Jackson, Nancy Johnson, Larry Lewin, Evie Matthews, Lesli Morrison, Betsy Shepard, and Barb Shirk. You have sheltered me, blessed me with the treasure of your friendship, and helped me hold hope in my heart.

And I also dedicate this work to Theresa and Timothy Shoemaker, my children. You have splashed my world with color and have brought me immeasurable joy and love. And to our beautiful cat, Pizza, who lays at my feet while I write.

Larry's Dedication

Para Robér
Un (he)rmano sin comparación

Table of Contents

Introduction xii
    "He's Teaching With a Full Deck" xii

Chapter One: An Introduction to Teaching With a Full Deck 1
    "An Ace in the Hole" 1
        Betty's Story 1
        What Is This Book About? 3
        Why This Book Now? 3
    So Off We Go! 4

Chapter Two: The Prepare Suit 7
    "Lay One's Cards on the Table" 7
        What's All This Talk About Suits? 7
        From Students to Teachers? 8
        There Are Always Nonconformists 10
        Let's Take a Theory Stop 10
    Some Prepare Tools 11
        The Open Mind and Adaptions 11
        Mental Floppy Disks 13
        Preview 14
        The Unit Organizer 17
        K-W-L and K-W-L Adaptations 20
        Personal Agendas and Work Plans 21
        Focus Questions to Elicit Content Knowledge 24
        Question Answer Relationship Strategy (QAR) ... 25
    Enough Already! 27

Chapter Three: Getting Started: The First Dare Suit **29**
   "Deal Me In" 29
      Larry's Story 29
   The First Dare 30
      My Reading—My Thinking Chart 31
      Double-Column Entry 33
      Through Thick and Thin 33
      SnapShots 36
      The ChecBric 40
      Storyboards 40
      Stick to It 44
      The Open Mind 45
      Click and Clunk 46
      Pocket Organizer 46
      Folded Bookmark 47
      Graphic Organizers (GOs) 48
      Get the Gist 51
      Theory Stop: The Importance of Constructing
         Meaning "From the Get Go" 51
   Conclusion 53

Chapter Four: The Repair Suit **55**
   "Playing It Close to the Chest, Hold One's Cards
     Close to the Vest" 55
      Betty's Story 55
      The Challenge of Addressing Misconceptions
        in the Classroom 56
      Theory Stop: Different Types of Knowledge 57
      Teaching and Repairing Procedural Knowledge 58
      Teaching and Repairing Declarative Knowledge ... 59
      Now Back to the Repair Tools 60
      When Inconsiderate Text Is the Issue 61
      When SocioCultural and/or Personal Beliefs
        Are Deeply Held 63
      When Naiveté Is the Issue 68
      When Inadequate Vocabulary Is the Issue 68
      Moving From the Minutiae to the Big Picture 69
      When the Locus of Attention Is Elsewhere 73
      When Faulty Teaching Is the Issue 76
   So, Where Are We Now? 76

Chapter Five: Share: Suit Show What You Are Learning ... **79**

"To Cash in One's Chips" ... 79
- Larry's Story ... 79
- Theory Stop: From the Saber-Toothed Curriculum to the Share Combo Special ... 80
- Writing to Share: "Info Out" ... 81
- More Formal Writing ... 88
- Technical Writing ... 94
- Fact to Fiction ... 96
- More Elaborate Writing: The Big Kahunas ... 98
- "Info Out" With Visuals ... 102
- "Info Out" by Speaking ... 108
- Sharing as Assessment ... 112

Conclusion ... 116

Chapter Six: What Works ... **119**

"Hold All the Aces" ... 119
- Betty's Story ... 119
- Students Hold All the Aces on the Effectiveness of Your Instruction ... 121
- A "Prepare" Theory Stop: Planning for Instruction ... 122

In Summary: Be a Data Nut ... 136

Chapter Seven: Teacher-to-Teacher ... **141**

"She's Teaching With a Full Deck" ... 141

Appendix ... **145**

About the Authors ... **171**

Index ... **173**

Acknowledgments

Betty's Acknowledgments

I would like to acknowledge the help of all the educators identified throughout this text for freely sharing examples of their work with us.

I would like to thank my program assistant, Darlene Deyo, for the care with which she approaches her work. Her support is critical to my success.

I would also like to thank the many children who have passed through my classrooms and from whom I have learned so much about teaching and learning. As Neil Postman states, "Children are the living messages we send to a time we will not see."[1]

And I am so thankful to have worked for over 33 years in Eugene Public School District 4J, Eugene, Oregon. It is such a fine school district, and I have had the opportunity to be creative and grow professionally in ways unimaginable!

Larry's Acknowledgments

An author of a book on teaching strategies is only the point-man for a team effort. Many people bestowed their ideas to contribute to this book.

First, a heartfelt thank you to the many teachers who shared their wonderful teaching techniques with me. They helped make me a better teacher, and they most certainly helped make this a better book.

---

[1] From *The Disappearance of Childhood*, published in 1982 by Vintage Books.

And of course, much gratitude to all the students whose work samples grace these pages. Without their work, the ideas presented would not be nearly as strong.

Also, thanks to Linda Barber, my wife, partner, and skilled copyeditor, for her hours and hours of assistance in preparing the manuscript.

Thanks to Sue Canavan, Executive Vice President of Christopher-Gordon Publishing, for suggesting this book, for helping us create it, and for guiding it to publication.

Finally, the greatest acknowledgment to Betty Shoemaker, colleague at the Eugene, Oregon, School District, copresenter at conferences, coauthor of this book, and most importantly, a longtime friend. Without her, this book could not have happened.

Introduction

"He's Teaching With a Full Deck"

The expression "playing with a full deck" literally means that the person is attempting to play a card game with a complete deck of cards. In this case, we use "teaching with a full deck" to mean a teacher is trained in and uses a full complement of teaching tools.

We are privileged to provide a lot of professional development to instructional staff. One day, a few years ago, after having just completed a presentation at a conference in Florida on performance-based assessment, we were walking around Disney World. The presentation had gone quite well. As we talked, we reflected on how our audiences described various but similar issues around instructional themes. These issues included

1. The dependence of many on the use of textbooks as the primary vehicle for instruction in spite of an intuitive sense that this did not always work well for students.

2. The fear that moving so consistently toward implementing standards-based systems would narrow the curriculum, focus on minutiae, and would force students, parents, and teachers into a "one size fits all" mentality.

3. The challenges of teaching students in the electronic age where they are becoming more and more conditioned to quick visual and sound bites, passive observation, and bathroom breaks every seven minutes to coincide with commercials.

4. The challenges of working with colleagues when many have, in their preservice training programs, received instruction in only "one right way to teach" or no instruction in the basics of good pedagogy.

5. The frustration of hearing students say—after what we perceive as our best efforts—"But I still don't get it!"

As we walked, we engaged in conversation about the importance of all teachers having access to many tools in order to effectively teach. These tools would move teachers away from over-dependence on textbooks, would allow for instruction that is differentiated for learners with different needs, and would provide the needed scaffolds for those students who "don't get it"—those who are currently underachieving.

Right then, we decided to commit ourselves to pulling together a number of strong instructional devices in one place and making them available to teachers. To that end, we have written this book.

As we began incorporating these tools into our staff development presentations, we settled on the idea of using the metaphor "teaching with a full deck." Interestingly, neither of us are card players. But we found teachers resonating with the full-deck notion. We have often joked with our colleagues that our first years of teaching could best be described as "teaching *without* a full deck"; that is, teaching without the methods to provide needed academic rigor while adequately addressing the varying needs of each of our students.

We are using the metaphor of "teaching with a full deck" not to imply insufficient mental capacity on the part of our teaching colleagues, but to reinforce the notion that all teachers need access to many tools in order to teach effectively. Just as a card player cannot be successful when missing a number of cards, teachers cannot be successful in increasing achievement of students with a wide spectrum of abilities, backgrounds, and interests when they are limited in the number of methods with which they can teach.

From that initial conversation, we have developed a series of actual teaching cards on which are recorded the tools described in this book. The tools can be used, with minor adaptations, at all grade levels K–12. We have introduced these tools to teachers across the nation and have collected examples of student work and teacher anecdotes about using most of the tools. And now, in this context, we introduce them to you. We include several examples at various grade levels to give you a sense of how you might be able to adapt them for your use. We do so in a teacher-to-teacher exchange, hoping they will help you and your colleagues "teach with a full deck."

CHAPTER
ONE

An Introduction to Teaching With a Full Deck

"An Ace in the Hole"

In the card game of poker, a card dealt face down and kept hidden is called a hole card, the most propitious card being the ace. An "ace in the hole" means that you have something that can supply a sure victory when revealed. We think that "teaching with a full deck" ensures victory—your "ace in the hole."

Betty's Story

Early last year, I went into the credit union where I do my banking. I had an appointment to meet with a loan officer about securing a loan on a new automobile. To my surprise, when the receptionist called me back to meet the loan officer, I found myself standing in front of one of my former first-grade students. Margot (I'll call her) looked up from her desk and said, "Mrs. Shoemaker! It's good to see you. You were my *favorite* teacher! How much money can I give you? (Pause...) *But,* if you would be more comfortable with another loan officer, I can arrange that."

"Of course not! After all of these years," I shared, "I *do* remember how well you did in math."

As I left the credit union that day, I thought a lot about my chance encounter. Soon my reflections turned to my first year of teaching. Maybe I *had* done a few things right. Margot had gotten a good start in a career where she uses math. But then I thought about some of my other students. What about little Jo Ann, who cried whenever I brought out the addition flash cards? Had I really done justice to *all* of my students?

Do you remember your first teaching assignment? Any happy memories? Any less than happy ones? How well did you perform?

I remember that first year well. I constrained myself from purchasing all the new and wonderful things I wanted—particularly a new car to replace the beat-up 1955 Chevy I drove—so that I could pay off my college loans. I would return home exhausted each evening to the little duplex I had rented. I slept on a borrowed sofa that folded out into a bed. I ate and worked on a card table that my folks had given me.

Most significantly, each day I would lug home my "bibles"—the myriad of teacher's guides and scope and sequence documents that the district had provided me with. I would eat dinner, clear off the dining table, such as it was, and spread out these critical resources in front of me. I tried to keep "ahead of the wave" each night by reading carefully and taking copious notes about what I would do first, next, and last in each of the upcoming day's lessons. I hadn't a clue what to do without these resources.

When I look back on those first years, I wonder if I did justice to my students having so few actual *teaching tools* from which to work. I soon came to discover that these "bibles" in some cases were, in fact, pulp fiction—poorly written, inconsistent in their approaches, and not very effective tools for designing lessons.

That first year I also had another reality hit me. Before I started teaching, I knew intellectually that my students would not all be alike. However, until my first year of teaching, I had no real conception of the wide range of abilities I would be addressing each day in the classroom. I found my limited methodology totally inadequate to address the very diverse needs of the myriad of individual students in my classroom.

I soon set out to find, create, and/or borrow teaching tools that I could master and that would give me an "instructional edge" with students. What do I mean by having an instructional edge? I mean that I wanted to have and use a cache of teaching methods that would help:

- Keep students *engaged* in the learning process;
- Help students *construct* more meaning around the content I was teaching;
- Address the needs of a *wide range* of student abilities; and
- Make it easier for students to *show me what they had learned* for assessment purposes.

What Is This Book About?

That is where this book comes in. It is a collection—a toolbox—of effective teaching methods. Over our many years of teaching, Larry and I have created or collected a large number of teaching tools that have proven to be effective in helping our students apply the key learning processes needed to acquire, and then share, content knowledge (facts, concepts, and generalizations). This book pulls together a large set of these methods in one place. Our goal is to provide you, the reader, with a number of methods to use in helping students more effectively use key processes to construct meaning around content knowledge from various subject disciplines at all grade levels.

Why This Book Now?

We like to say that we have a bulimic history of curriculum and instruction in education in the United States. This is a rather graphic metaphor to use, but it makes our point. What is bulimia? Bulimia is an eating disorder marked by excessive eating binges, followed by self-induced purging.[1] At times, we educators have gone on wild teaching binges in which we indulged in the "one right way to view curriculum" or the "one right teaching method." After a wave of a particular teaching binge, we have purged our instructional programs of it and moved on to another binge, using another equally touted method. Many tenured teachers nod their heads in acknowledgment when we describe this. They laughingly share the binges in their own teaching careers, along with caricatures of those tried and true staff developers who pushed each method.

Let us make it explicitly clear here: There is no one right way to teach, just as there is no one right approach to healthy eating. Instead, there are many right ways to teach. Teachers should be trained in the use of a wide range of methods. They should also receive training in how to draw from their large teaching tool repertoire and select appropriate methods to use in a particular instructional setting. Educators who embrace the "one right way" notion are caught up in an unhealthy instructional pattern in the same way bulimics are caught up in an unhealthy approach to eating. Good teaching involves the use of numerous methods, strategies, and tactics—a "full deck."

Secondly, it is important to acknowledge that, in most cases, each of these binges we have experienced in education has brought some strong elements into the curriculum and instruction diet of teachers. These elements should not be discarded as the new wave begins, but instead should be incorporated into the teaching "deck of cards" along with previously learned cards and should be played at the appropriate times in a course or unit. We shouldn't abandon tried and true practices when a new approach is developed.

A third point is important to make here. As we are well aware, most states by now have embraced some form of a standards-based system. That is, clear academic content standards have been published and students are held accountable to demonstrate competency around these standards. Students demonstrate competency by taking secured assessment tests at the local or state level and better yet, in some cases, through the production of classroom-based performance tasks. As we interact with teachers throughout the United States, Mexico, and Canada, most agree that they support the notion of holding students to high standards; and in most cases, they appreciate the clarity that the published content standards bring to the day-to-day instructional program. However, almost with one voice, teachers share their need for additional teaching tools that can assist more students in achieving these high academic standards. Embracing a standards-based system requires students to move beyond rote facts and to demonstrate competence in a myriad of application-based efforts in reading, writing, speaking, and mathematics. Teachers are then challenged to adapt their instructional programs to incorporate more contextual-based teaching and learning, more substantive dialogue with students as they progress, and more hands-on, activity-based units of study. This book includes a number of tools that will help educators do this.

And the last point to make here is the notion that this book is primarily about tools for teaching. We recognize that some of these tools can serve a dual purpose in that they can be used as forms of formative and summative evaluation. It is important to remember that instruction and assessment *are* inextricably linked. By all means, use the information you collect from using the tools to help you assess student growth.[2]

So Off We Go!

Our goal, then, is to equip instructional staff with a large repertoire of methods to use in helping students more effectively construct meaning around content knowledge from various disciplines. We want the reader to know that the emphasis in this book will not be on understanding and learning one particular elaborate instructional program or product—although we will introduce you to elements of certain systems. Instead, the emphasis will be to facilitate teacher-to-teacher exchanges of practical, hands-on tools that can easily be adapted to each reader's own specific teaching setting. That is, we will share tools that improved our teaching and our students' learning.

In each chapter of this book, we will share with teachers a set of "teaching cards" in each of four suits. Each card will describe how to use the method as well as give suggestions for how the method can be adapted for lower performing, academically challenged, and gifted students. Because instruction and assessment are inextricably linked, these tools, in many cases, can be used for both. After reading the book, each reader will have acquired a deck of "teaching cards" from which to draw when designing units.

The chapters are organized in the same way we try to organize the teaching of an instructional unit: (a) *Prepare,* (b) *First Dare,* (c) *Repair,* and (d) *Share.*

Chapter 2: The Prepare Suit

In the next chapter, chapter 2, our focus will be on Prepare tools—tools to use when preparing students for taking in new information. We will describe several instructional/assessment tools that help students tap their existing knowledge. These tools will also serve as miniassessments that the teacher can use as a quick diagnostic device to shape the lessons in the unit. Chapter 2 will also emphasize the role of questioning in the classroom. Several methods will be introduced to create effective focus questions for units and courses, as well as tips for how to engage all students in substantive dialogue throughout the unit.

Chapter 3: The First Dare Suit

In this chapter, we will introduce the reader to various instructional methods that help make their First Dare to learning new information. These methods help students process new information as they take it in—organizing and integrating new knowledge into existing schemas. In chapter 3, we will also describe how to identify and to more effectively select and use appropriate print and nonprint resources, including identifying considerate and inconsiderate materials, and modifying resources to make them more accessible to special needs students.

Chapter 4: The Repair Suit

Chapter 4 will introduce the reader to the Repair Suit—instructional methods that help students synthesize and extend their initial conceptual understanding to improve comprehension of the content, as well as helping students rid themselves of persistent misconceptions.

Chapter 5: The Share Suit

Chapter 5 will describe several tools to use with students to help them share the knowledge they have gained throughout the instructional unit; that is, apply newly learned content in real-life situations where the audience is larger than the teacher.

About Wild Cards

Throughout chapters 2 through 5, we will share a number of *Wild Cards*—tools that can be used all the time—before, during, and after the lesson or unit. These *Wild Cards* are somewhat like the jokers in the card deck. We labeled them *Wild Cards* because of their applicability as a *Prepare* tool, a *First Dare* tool, a *Repair* tool, and/or a *Share* tool all combined into one.

Chapter 6: What Works

What works and what doesn't work—conducting simple action research in one's classroom to determine the effectiveness of various methods will be the focus of this chapter. Readers will be encouraged to give various tools a try in their classrooms and to track the effectiveness of each. We end with a strong recommendation to continue to use classroom-based action research to constantly improve one's pedagogy.

Chapter 7: Teacher-to-Teacher

In this chapter, our colleague and friend, Kay Mehas, interviews us. We wrap up the book by reviewing the key points about teaching with a full toolkit as described throughout the previous chapters.

End Notes

1. Braham, C. G. (Ed.). (1998). *Random house webster's dictionary,* New York: Ballentine Books.

2. The reader is encouraged to read our book titled, *Great performances: Creating classroom-based assessment tasks,* for more detailed information on classroom-based assessment.

CHAPTER
TWO

The Prepare Suit

"Lay One's Cards on the Table"

To lay one's cards on the table is to show your hand. In poker, when the bets are final, the remaining players show their cards. Teachers are encouraged to deal their teaching devices openly and honestly. They need to lay all of their cards on the table and strategically select the best tools to use at any stage in the lesson or unit.

What's All This Talk About Suits?

Before we launch into introducing you to some new teaching tools, it will be helpful to share with you the basic "suits" in our "full teaching deck." We named them after Larry's generic four-step tool for teaching the process approach: Prepare, First Dare, Repair, and Share.

These four generic steps or stages are used in teaching students to use the process approach with any process. They serve to guide novice learners through any demanding operation. They are identified as the behaviors that experts actually apply when using each process. These four distinct, yet overlapping, stages involve: (a) thinking and planning before actually beginning, (b) first attempting to implement the plan, (c) evaluating the results for possible improvement, and (d) presenting, using, and/or sharing the results. For simplicity and easy recall, students are taught the steps as presented in Figure 2.1.

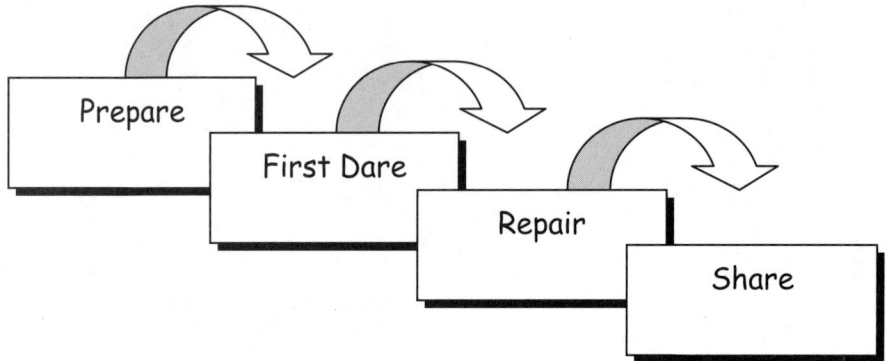

Figure 2.1   Teaching the process approach using a generic template

It should be noted that the four-step Prepare, First Dare, Repair, and Share template was designed to provide beginners with a predictable plan of attack. This plan may seem familiar to you. It was developed to reflect processes you may already be teaching, such as the writing process, the classic scientific method, or open-ended problem solving in mathematics.

Of course, as students become increasingly familiar and proficient with these generic steps, like experts they will adapt, streamline, and personalize them. These four steps rhyme to help students remember them. The steps have been successfully taught to learners in the primary grades, intermediate grades, middle school, and high school.

To understand this four-step tool, one must first understand the difference between processes, strategies, and skills. *Processes* are frameworks for approaching difficult operations—a user's overall game plan. They imply a predictable application of a series of steps to achieve a goal or a particular result. They involve actions that engage the use of skills and/or strategies in combination. *Strategies* comprise a menu of skills that can be used in a particular step of a process. *Skills* are learned abilities, proficiencies, and dexterities that are used in combination with other skills as a part of a strategy; skills determine how successful the use of the strategy will be.[1] To summarize, strategies incorporating the use of specific skills must be applied consistently in various steps of a process to achieve the desired results.

From Students to Teachers?

As we taught our own students to use the Prepare, First Dare, Repair, and Share template, we began to articulate and teach particular strategies and skills tied to each step in the process. Even though some strategies are unique to a given process, we noticed that a number of strategies were commonly used in more than one process. Figure 2.2 summarizes these common strategies into families.

Prepare Strategies

Surveying:	Used to take stock of presented information and relationships
Retrieving:	Used to tap prior knowledge about a topic from one's memory
Planning:	Used to complete a project in a timely manner
Forecasting:	Used to anticipate potential learning through predicting or questioning

First Dare Strategies

Focusing:	Used to selectively attend to significant information
Information gathering:	Used to acquire needed new information
Self regulating:	Used to monitor one's own construction of meaning (metacognition)
Generating:	Used to produce new information, meanings, or ideas
Organizing:	Used to track data, construct meaning, and enhance retention

Repair Strategies

Fixing-up:	Used to resolve any cognitive dissonance
Evaluating:	Used to assess the value, quality or significance of ideas
Analyzing:	Used to examine essential features as parts of the whole
Perspective-taking:	Used to examine other points of view

Share Strategies

Integrating:	Used to synthesize, connect, and combine information meaningfully
Organizing:	Used to structure large amounts of data meaningfully for presentations
Presenting:	Used to develop a final product using various media

Figure 2.2 A list of strategy families tied to various steps in a process

Once we became clearer about the clusters of strategies we wanted students to learn to use routinely, we began to develop a set of teaching tools that would help us teach these particular strategies. It is one thing to expose a student to a particular learning strategy; however, it is quite another to have a student integrate it routinely into his or her repertoire of learning tools.

Even students report that "strategies" are critical to learning. In a study of students in one of our high schools, high-achieving students described the strategies they routinely used in and out of class to complete schoolwork confidently and successfully. So in this chapter, we are going to introduce you to some new teaching tools that will help you teach students to use Prepare strategies routinely and independently. Let us lay our Prepare cards on the table for you to see and possibly adopt.

There Are Always Nonconformists

As we described on page 6, some tools we liked could be used before, during, and after the lesson or unit. These tools are useful in all the stages—Prepare, First Dare, Repair, and Share. We call them Wild Cards—somewhat like the jokers in a card deck.

Let's Take a Theory Stop

Meet another type of card in our card deck. We call them *Theory Stop* cards. Theory Stop cards aren't members of any particular suit. They are a little like the "Instructions" cards included in many card games. While cards that include the instructions for how to play a game are not used in actually playing the game, they provide helpful background information about the game. In the same way, Theory Stop cards provide background information, research, and rationale for using the other cards.

Why Theory Stop? Our friend and colleague, Dr. Joseph Dimino, describes theory stops in this way: A driver on the stock car racing circuit takes a "pit stop" after so many laps around the track. The driver does this to stock up on racing supplies, including new tires and fuel. We, too, as teachers need to take a pit stop by pulling in from the track of teaching to review the literature on the latest teaching and learning research.

A Theory Stop: Teachers Really Make a Difference

In the last two decades, educational researchers have increasingly focused on classroom-level factors that enhance or inhibit student achievement. Wright, Horn, Sanders (1997)[2] analyzed achievement scores of about 60,000 students in Grades 3–5 in five subject areas (mathematics, reading, language arts, social studies, and science). The study documented that the most important factor affecting student achievement is *the teacher*. They reinforce that if student achievement is to improve, schools must invest in the improvement of teachers. They go on to state that effective teachers appear to be effective with students of all achievement levels—even in classes with varying levels of heterogeneity. Marzano (2003),[3] in his recently published book, *What Works in Schools: Translating Research into Action,* shares a number of research studies and their implications for educational practice. He draws from the work of William Sanders and his colleagues (Sanders & Horn, 1994;[4] Wright, Horn, & Sanders, 1997), as summarized by Kati Haycock,[5] and graphically represents achievement gains for students in least effective and most effective teachers' classrooms. "On the average, the most effective teachers produced gains of about 53 percentage points in student achievement over one year, whereas the least effective teachers produced achievement gains of about 14 percentage points over one year. To understand these results, consider the fact that researchers estimate that students typically gain about 34 percentile points in achievement during one academic year."[6] He continues with his analysis by showing that the cumulative effect over a three-year period is sizable for students having most effective teachers. Students with the most effective teachers make a gain of 83 percentile points, while students who have the least effective teachers over the course of three years will make only a 29 percentile gain.

As we begin introducing you to a number of Prepare tools, we want you to remember that, *without a doubt,* what you choose to do in the classroom makes a difference! Having a large repertoire of methods from which to draw and using these methods strategically can, and does, make a difference.

Some Prepare Tools

So let's launch into the Prepare suit and learn some excellent tools for helping students prepare to take in new information. And as we go, we will throw in a few Wild Cards along the way.

The Open Mind and Adaptations

An effective Prepare tool, the *Open Mind,* is one we have consistently used (see Figure 2.3). The notion is to get students to open up their minds and share what they are currently thinking about any given subject.

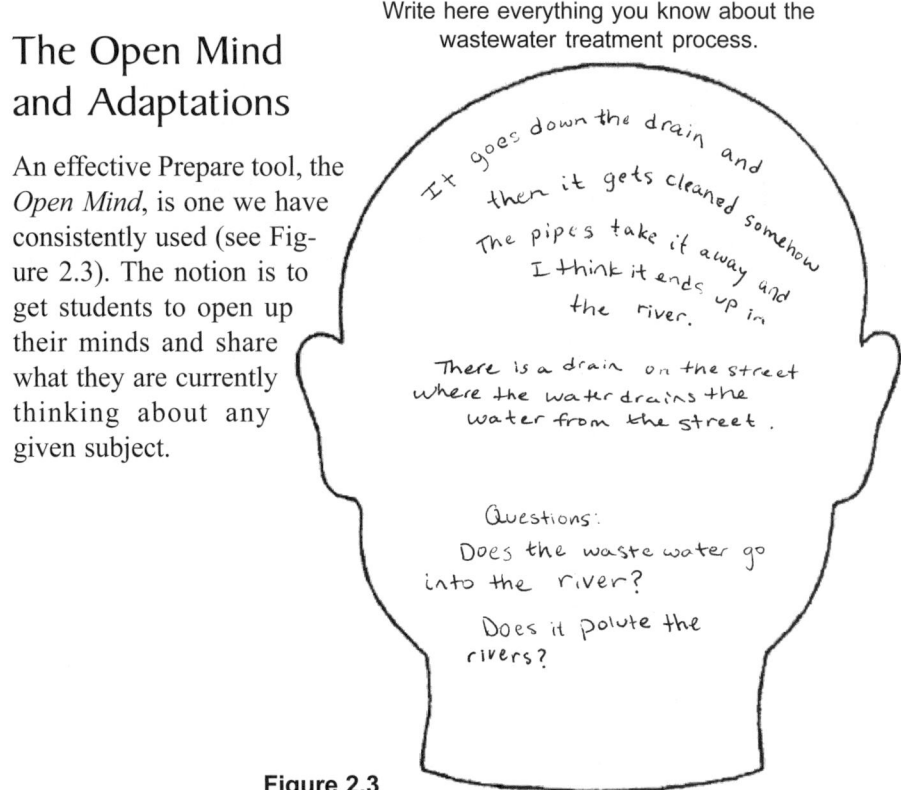

Figure 2.3
Theresa's open mind on the wastewater treatment process

Students often inform us that they think classroom work is a game—a game in which the teacher has the "right" answer in his/her mind, and the role of the student is to go on a quest to provoke the teacher into supplying this right answer. After the right answer is revealed, it then becomes the goal of the students to memorize the right answer so that it can be brought back up (regurgitated) at test time.

Again, many students believe we teachers are not really interested in what they are thinking. They believe that we are only interested in continuing to play the game. Our goal is to convince our students of the exact opposite; that is, that we are genuinely interested in what they are thinking about the subject so that we can help them refine that thinking. The Open Mind is one retrieving tool you can use to do this.

Give each student a copy of a blank open mind. Ask students to record, using pictures or words, anything that comes to mind about the subject. Provide assistance to students as needed to motivate them to reveal as many ideas as they can generate.

As the teacher, what could you do with these open minds? Scan them as a diagnostic device to identify any common themes, any common misconceptions, and/or any major information gaps. Then plan your instruction accordingly.

The Open Mind tool can be used again at the end of a unit or course as an integrating strategy. And likewise, the Open Mind can be used in the First Dare stage as a "disguised" notetaking device. For example, during the viewing of a video, ask students to complete an Open Mind on the key points shared in the video. (We have noticed that when students are assigned notetaking during the learning of new content, they groan; however, when assigned to fill in an Open Mind during the First Dare stage of learning new content, we rarely hear complaints.) Compare the before and after results to assess growth in conceptual understanding.

Of course, teachers freely make adaptations or modifications of the Open Mind to fit their own instructional context. For example, Figure 2.4 shows one teacher's adaptation—the *Open Turtle*. As suggested above, she shifted the use of the Open Turtle and used it as a *First Dare* tool. Students recorded

Figure 2.4 The open turtle

their reflections on a folk tale as they were reading. Figure 2.5 shows another teacher's adaptation—the *Brainy Light Bulb*. Students used the light bulb before reading the chapter. The teacher instructed them to scan the chapter and respond to the prompts on the light bulb as they scanned.

Mental Floppy Disks

In our book, *Great Performances,*[7] we described other adaptations of the Open Mind. They included recording on an outline of the actual head of a historical figure or character, as well as using a totally different shape. Here is one more example of an Open Mind adaptation. We call it the *Mental Floppy Disk* and it is illustrated in Figure 2.6.

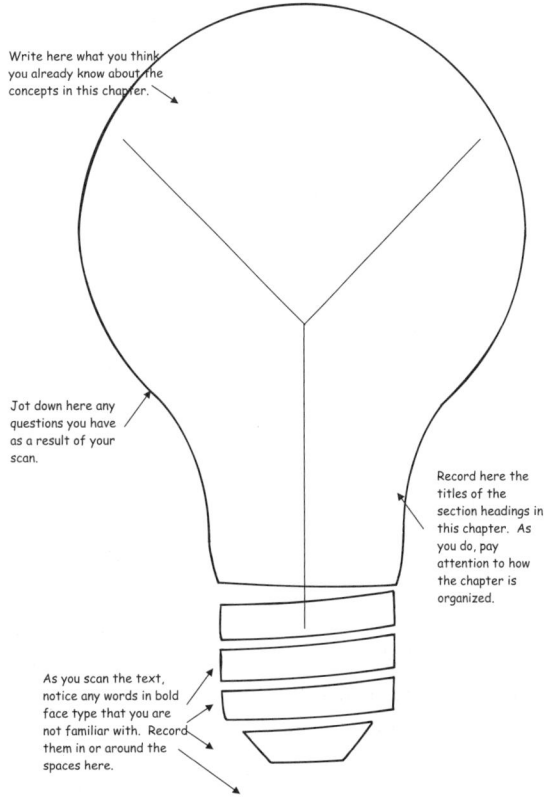

Figure 2.5 The brainy light bulb

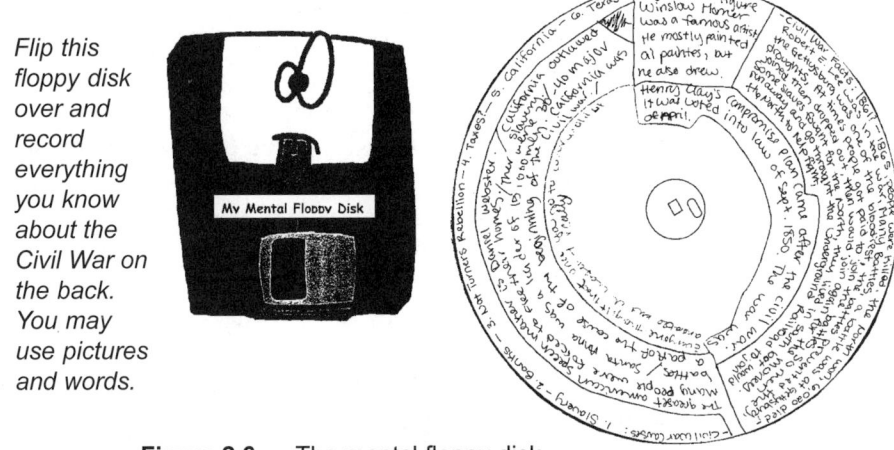

Figure 2.6 The mental floppy disk

Larry shares with students, "Kids, I have some great news! Your brains are ultrafast computers. However, I don't have access to the content information you have saved on your internal hard drive (C: Drive). So help me out here. Download what is in your brain about this topic on this mental floppy disk. Be sure to include everything that comes into your mind, using words, images, or both." Using both text and graphic images provides more options for students to get all of their ideas down.

It is important to note that this retrieving strategy, like all other retrieving strategies, is designed to get at both conceptions *and* misconceptions about the topic of study before the unit starts. It is imperative that you scan the material "stored" on the mental floppy disks before you start your instruction. Because these tools reveal misconceptions and information gaps, you must address them explicitly in your instruction during the course of the unit. For those of you on the cutting edge of technology, you could upgrade the Mental Floppy Disk to "Burn me a CD" of your thinking.

Preview

Preview is a Prepare tool used before reading a text. Janette Klingner and Sharon Vaughn, as a part of the Collaborative Strategic Reading (CSR) program, developed it.[8] CSR combines both reading strategy instruction and cooperative learning to increase comprehension in content area textbooks. Students work in small, cooperative groups to assist one another in applying four reading strategies to increase their comprehension. We will introduce you to the first of these strategies, Preview, here. When previewing, a student is taught to scan the text (surveying) to generate interest and questions (forecasting) about the text to be read, retrieve any background knowledge (retrieving) about the subject, and make predictions (forecasting) about what might be learned.

As the teacher, share with your class that strong readers always preview the text before reading. When one previews, one scans and skims the text (looks at the title, subheadings, and pictures) to get a sense of what the chapter/section/unit might be about. One also ponders what one might already know about the topic. And one makes predictions about what one might learn from reading. Figure 2.7 shows our adaptation of the Preview tool—the *CSR Learning Log*.

We have students take 3 to 4 minutes to scan and skim. We then give them about five minutes to record any ideas. For students just learning the Preview tool, structure the recording activity by having students move systematically through each column. Then have them join a small group, share ideas, and add to their log.

Even though the Preview tool here was developed specifically for use in reading, teachers have modified it for use in other contexts, including before viewing a video and before listening to an oral presentation.

The Prepare Suit 15

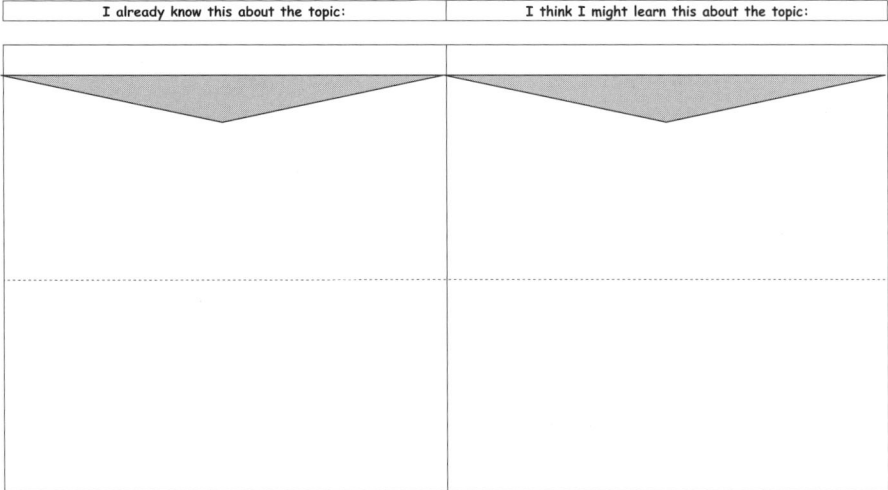

Figure 2.7 The CSR learning log

A Preview of Coming Attractions

Betty developed this multimedia tool to provide students with a preview of the unit as a whole and to provide a print document on which to record notes as the unit progresses. It was created in Microsoft PowerPoint® and then projected onto a screen as an introduction to the unit. PowerPoint® allows one to view the slides through a projection device. One can also create colored overheads of each slide. Figure 2.8 provides thumbnails of six slides in the presentation.

Another PowerPoint® feature allows you to print up notes pages with the slide itself sitting at the top of the page and then blank space for recording notes. I print the blank notes pages and then have students use them as a retrieving strategy, a planning strategy, or as an information gathering and organizing strategy. Figure 2.9 is an example of the notes taken by one young woman in this American Literature class. The *Preview of Coming Attractions* gives each student a behind-the-scenes look at the unit as a whole.

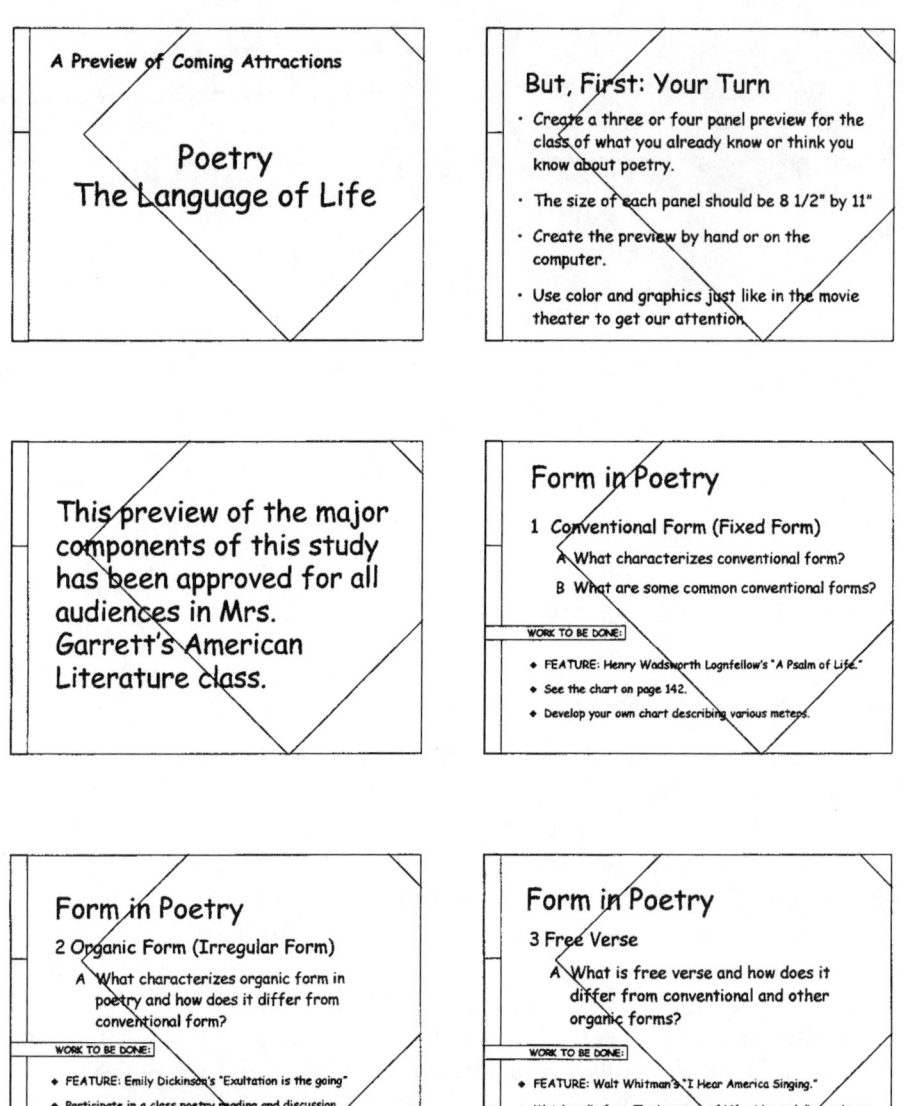

Figure 2.8 Thumbnails of the Preview of Coming Attractions

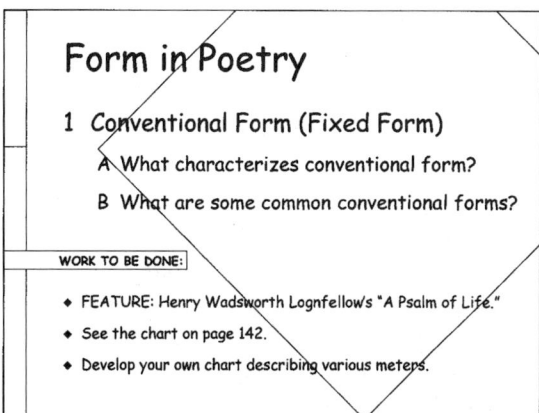

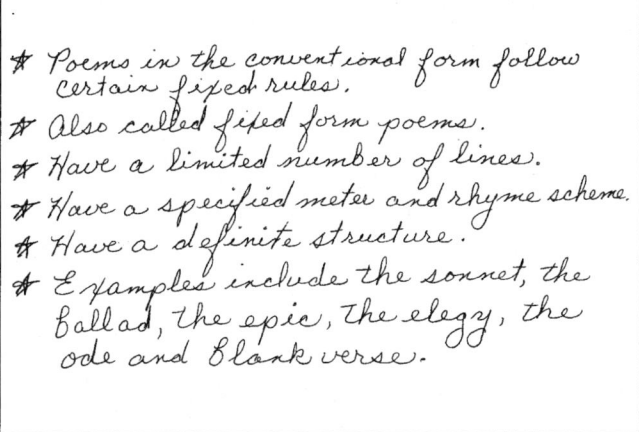

Figure 2.9 Notes Page Example

The Unit Organizer

One of the social science standards in our district at the third-grade level is "Students are able to give examples of how local government does or does not provide for needs and wants of its citizens." In teaching a course addressing this standard, teachers help students become familiar with various needs and wants that citizens have including:

- the need for police, fire, and emergency services;
- the need for transportation networks;
- the need to provide clean water to citizens and to treat waste water; and
- the desire to provide library, aquatics, and other cultural services to the community.

In a context such as this, we encourage teachers to use a very powerful instructional tool called the *Unit Organizer Routine*. Keith Lenz and his colleagues at the University of Kansas Center for Research on Learning developed this routine.[9] This content enhancement routine is designed to enable students who have been at risk for failure in school to acquire and use helpful strategies in learning school material. In our experience, we have found the Unit Organizer Routine to be of great value to students of varying ability levels. The strength of the Unit Organizer Routine is that it provides students with a picture of what's to come—it frames the unit. Wouldn't it be nice if *all* of our students came to school hard-wired to mentally organize the unit before it starts? Chances are they need some help. So read on.

We have labeled the Unit Organizer Routine as a Wild Card because of its applicability not only at the Prepare stage but also at the First Dare, Repair, and Share stages. However, we place it here among other Prepare tools because of its use of critical retrieving and planning strategies—first for the teacher and then for the students (see Figure 2.2).

Lenz defines a unit as "any chunk of content that a teacher selects to organize information into lessons and that ends in some type of test or closure activity."[10] A course of study is usually made up of two, three, or four units. The Unit Organizer Routine is used to help students: "(a) understand how the unit can be part of bigger course ideas or a sequence of units, (b) see a method for organizing knowledge, (c) define the relationships associated with knowledge, (d) clarify what has been done in relation to what must be done, (e) monitor progress and accomplishments in learning, and (f) recognize what has been learned through self-questioning. In general, the Unit Organizer can be used to help students become oriented to where they *are,* and where they *are going* in learning."[11]

The teacher uses the Unit Organizer to do initial unit planning and then introduces the unit to students. (See a graphic representation of the front side of a completed Unit Organizer in Figure 2.10.)

Each student is provided with a blank Unit Organizer. The teacher writing on a blank overhead walks students through each numbered step on the Unit Organizer. Students record as they go. Even though the teacher has prepared a draft of the Unit Organizer in advance, the goal is to assist students to coconstruct one together to enhance their engagement in the learning to come.

The Unit Organizer has three particularly notable features. First, notice the unit map marked as step 5. The unit map serves as a graphic representation of how the unit will be organized. (For more information on using graphic organizers in your classroom, refer to chapter 3 in our book, *Great Performances*.[12])

Second, note step 7, the unit self-test questions. The answers to these questions, jointly crafted by the teacher and the students, reflect the major concepts developed during the unit and the relationships of these concepts to one another. Third, the unit schedule, marked step 8 on the organizer, provides a place

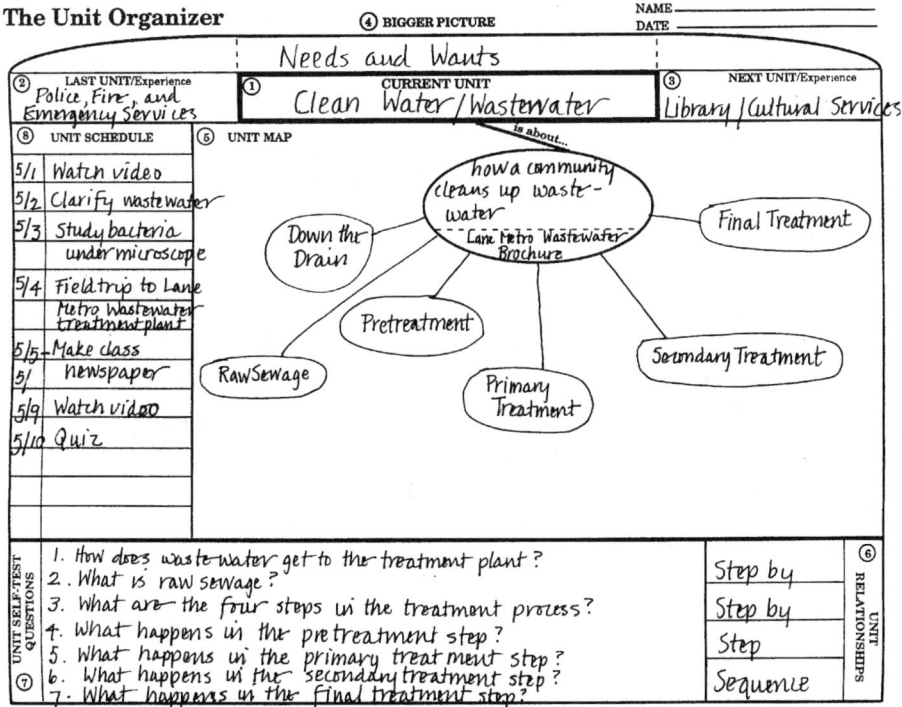

Figure 2.10 The unit organizer routine (front)

to list the assignments, activities, quizzes, and tests that are to be completed during the unit. A dotted line can be added just to the right of each assignment, leaving a place for students to check off each assignment as it is completed. Some teachers have used this space instead to add point values to each assignment listed as a way to rank order the importance of each in the overall context of the unit. When items are completed, students are given the appropriate number of points as a part of the grading.

Following the completion of the front side of the Unit Organizer as a class, the teacher facilitates a brief review of the main elements of the unit. Students are then instructed to place their own copy at the front of their working folders or binders. As the unit progresses, students use the expanded unit map on the flip side for taking notes and creating graphic representations of the critical subtopics in the unit, as well as adding any key vocabulary that is taught throughout the unit (see Figure 2.11).

At the end of the unit, students use the Unit Organizer as a study guide in preparing for the final project or unit test. The reader is challenged to use the Unit Organizer here to identify the differences between floaters, sinkers, and lurkies.

Why is the Unit Organizer Routine such a powerful teaching and learning tool? First, the Unit Organizer formally structures the use of planning and fore-

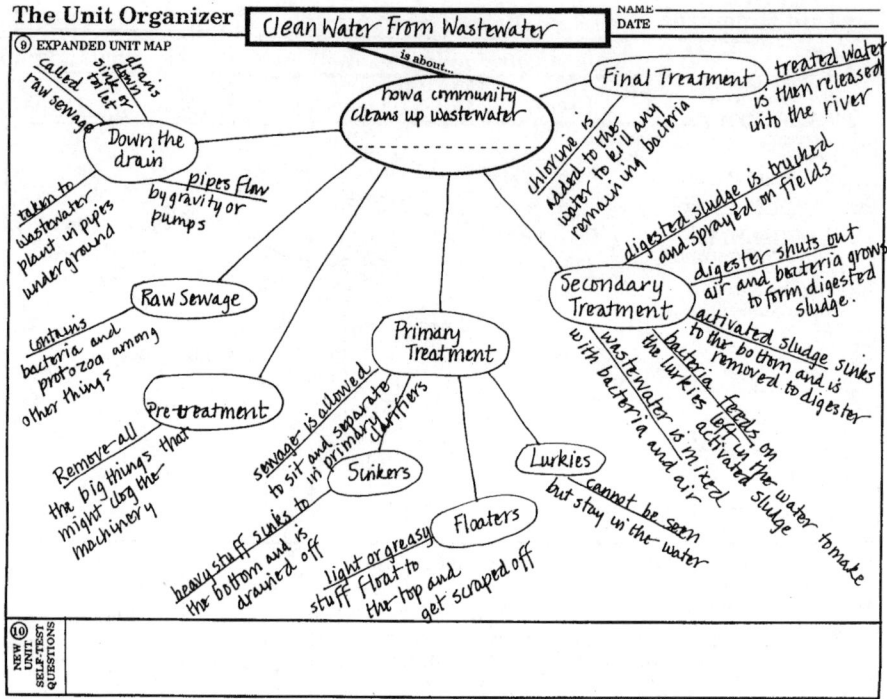

Figure 2.11 The unit organizer routine (back)

casting strategies as Prepare tools for the unit ahead. It also includes a graphic organizer as an effective organizing strategy and then uses the graphic organizer to help students analyze the relationship of parts to the whole throughout the unit. Finally, at the end of the unit, the Unit Organizer serves as a study guide, an integrating strategy, to pull it all together.[13]

K-W-L and K-W-L Adaptations

Another wild card a teacher can use to teach students content knowledge is the *K-W-L* activity. Donna Ogle developed this Prepare through Share tool.[14] It has been used for a number of years and is the grand momma of many other retrieving tools.

The letters stand for what I **K**now, what I **W**ant to know, and what I have **L**earned. Students record this information in a three-column chart either as a class or individually. In column one, the students apply a retrieving strategy and list everything they know about the topic. In column two, they apply a forecasting strategy and list what they would like to learn. Many teachers have students forecast by writing column two statements in the form of questions. And in column three, students record what they learn. The tool then becomes a great integrating strategy to help students pull key unit ideas together in one place.

Many variations of the K-W-L have been developed. They include creating a *K-W-H-L* chart, adding the **H** for **H**ow I will learn; or a *K-W-W-L* chart adding the second **W** for **W**here I will locate the information. Another variation is the *K-W-L-S* chart, adding the **S** for what I **S**till want to learn. A fourth is the *K-T-W-L* chart, where students list in column one the things they **K**now, in column two the things they **T**hink they know but are not positive about, in column three what they **W**ant to learn, and in column four what they have **L**earned. See Figure 2.12 for an example of a *K-W-H-L* completed as a part of the Needs and Wants unit described in the Unit Organizer Routine above.

What We Know About Needs and Wants	What We Want to Learn about Needs and Wants	How We Will Learn About Needs and Wants	What We Learned about Needs and Wants
• Need food • Need shelter • Need clothing • Need entertainment • Need and want friendship • Need to be not to hot or too cold • Need money • Need medicines • Need transportation • Want cell phones • Want candy • Want nice cars • Want to win the lottery • Want to go to Disneyland • Want good health • Want friends • Want a husband or wife • Want more free time • Want to play	Want to know: • how to get nice things • how to get a job Want to learn: • how to build houses • how to get a skateboard or scooter park built by our school • how 911 works • how to ride the city bus • how to keep food safe	• We will read our Social Studies book • We will visit city hall • We will study the bus map • We will do a Web search • We will watch a movie • We will take a bus ride	We learned: • The city charges people taxes to pay for services like policemen, firemen, and meter maids. • There are different departments in the city. Each department has a certain job like keeping the streets clean or like running the library. • The bus system is complex and meets downtown every so many minutes. • Firemen and policemen do other jobs than catching robbers or putting out fires – jobs like speaking in schools. • Sinkers, floaters, and lurkies are the raw sewage that comes into the wastewater treatment plant and are removed from the water. • We learned about how neighborhood groups can get the city council to build things in their neighborhood.

Figure 2.12 A class-created K-W-H-L on needs and wants

Personal Agendas and Work Plans

Here is an effective planning strategy to help your students be more successful in directing their own learning. The *Agenda* is critical for completing daily assignments and the lengthier substantive *Share* projects, which we will discuss in more detail in chapter 5. Agendas are step-by-step work plans that specify what a particular student must complete in a specified time. Student agendas throughout a class may be identical or may have dissimilar elements in them to accommodate the needs of different learners. Figure 2.13 provides a model of one student's personal agenda. This sample was developed by Carol Ann Tomlinson at the University of Virginia, and is called the *Personal Agenda*.[15]

You may have students determine the order in which they will complete agenda items, or you may prescribe the order and time frames in which each agenda item will be completed. Set aside a little time each day to review agendas.

While students work on the tasks on their agendas, you can pull together small groups of students who need guided work or direct instruction with a particular concept or skill.

Personal Agenda for: ____________________
Starting Date: ____________________

Initial here when complete	Task	Special Instructions

Figure 2.13 The personal agenda

We prefer to call these agendas *Work Plans,* and have adapted them to help younger students complete in-class independent work without the direct and *constant* supervision of the teacher. Figure 2.14 provides an example of a class period-by-class period work plan for Grade 4 students to complete an in-class, pop-up book summarizing their reading of the book, *Shiloh,* by Phyllis Reynolds Naylor.[16]

As you can see, the teacher, Mary Jane Goewey, specified how much time was allotted for each task and also included the materials the student would need to gather to complete the task. She reported that using work plans has consistently increased her students' completion of assignments and projects in and out of class. This has been particularly true for those learners who come to school with no apparent understanding or abilities to plan out and

Work Plan for Shiloh
Planner: Daniel

Date	Time	GOAL	Materials	Accomplished YES!	no
10/9	40	Open mind / goal sheet	book paper	☆	
10/10	30	cover assemble book	book stuff	✓	
10/10	40	Spiral - Setting (edited) Title page	Spiral, art stuff	✓	
10/11	30	final setting protagonist (edit)	"	✓	
10/11	40	antagonist (edit) art for pro. + ant.	"	✓	
10/12	30	pro. + ant. / finals conflict / resolution	"	✓	
10/16	30	favorite part (edit) art for c/r + fav. part	"	✓	
10/16	40	final fav. part art for fav. part	"	✓	
10/17	30	recommendation (edit) art for recom.	"	✓	
10/17	40	final recom. finish up	"	✓	

Figure 2.14 Shiloh work plan

complete projects over time. Too many students fail because no one has *ever* taught them to plan out and complete a project from start to finish.

Many of our middle and high school colleagues use a computer-generated or handwritten calendar as a Work Plan. Again, students are required to keep these work plans in the front of their binders to reference as the unit progresses. Figure 2.15 provides the reader with an example of a calendar work plan developed by our colleague, Franzi Thompson, for use in her fourth-year Spanish class at South Eugene High School. Note that Franzi coded the work each day with a T for "la tarea" (homework), a C for "el cuaderno" (notebook), and an L for "el libro de texto" (textbook).

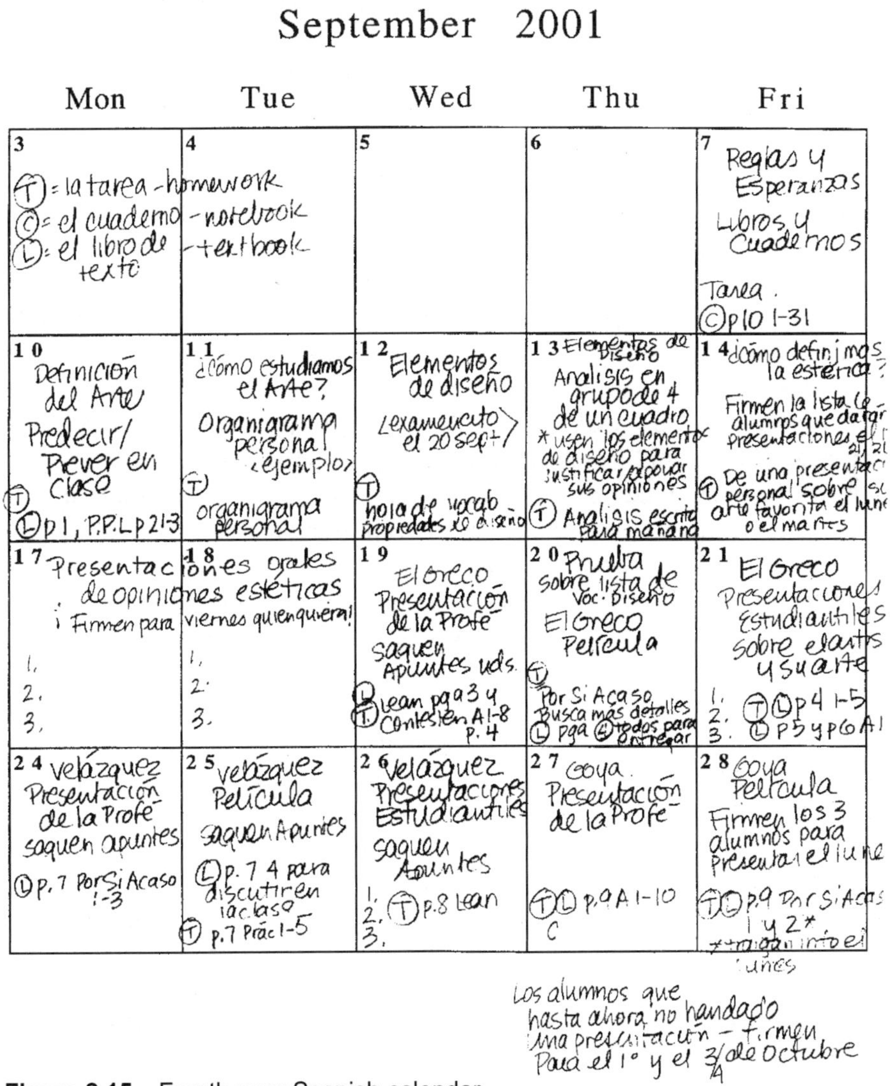

Figure 2.15 Fourth-year Spanish calendar work plan

We bet you are asking, "What happens with those students who don't complete the work in the specified period of time?" First, many teachers report that they have students complete the agenda/work plan in pencil, in case the time allocations and dates need to be adjusted. In the example in Figure 2.15, Ms. Goewey reported that the few students who were unable to complete the project in the time allotted took the work home to finish as homework. Other teachers report that they build a short time in each day—variously called "Hodge Podge" time or "Ketchup" time (AKA "Catch Up" time)—for students to complete projects when they need a little additional time. Flexibility is the key.

Focus Questions to Elicit Content Knowledge

Questions play an important role in the development of student thinking and learning. Focus questions can empower students to become active producers of their own knowledge, rather than passive consumers of the knowledge prepared and presented by the teacher. That is, they put the student in the *driver's seat*. Teachers, have you noticed recently that when you go home on Friday night you want to *crash* while your students go home and want to GO OUT? What is wrong with this picture? Teachers plan the instructional trip and all too often they take the instructional trip by themselves, doing all the driving while their students sit passively in the back seats or impatiently kick the back of the front seats waiting for the trip to be over.

Do you work with a textbook that lists the key concepts to be learned on the first page of each unit? Some students simply memorize this list, wait the unit out, and then regurgitate the list back to you on the unit test. We often suggest to teachers that they cover up the key concept section at the front of the unit and replace it with a listing of the key questions to be answered by the students as they complete the unit. Tell students—all of whom love to drive or can't wait to drive—"Hey, you are in the driver's seat. Go out and find the answers to these questions!"

Besides putting a kid in the driver's seat, questions do two other critical things. They are critical to the Prepare strategy of *forecasting*. And focus questions focus learners to "selectively attend" to significant information in the next stage in the process—the First Dare stage (see Figure 2.2).

Dr. Sandra Kaplan, a nationally known leader in talented and gifted education, has helped shape our thinking about the critical role questioning plays in the Prepare stage of any process. In *The Grid: A Model to Construct Differentiated Curriculum for the Gifted*,[17] Kaplan describes how to effectively construct good key focus questions. They are constructed by using key words and concepts in combination. Figure 2.16 lists key words for developing strong focus questions.

• kinds	• importance	• evolution
• types	• consequence	• style
• conditions	• characteristics	• time (past, present, future)
• significant	• purpose	• cause and effect
• relationship	• function	• value

Figure 2.16 Key words to develop focus questions

The following are sample focus questions written to develop the concepts of communities and change:

- What *kinds* of communities are found in _____?
- How have communities *evolved* as a consequence of _____?
- In what ways is _____ *important* in a community?
- What are the *characteristics* of a _____ community?
- What are the *conditions* that create change in _____?
- What changes are represented by the *evolution* of _____?
- In what ways has change been *important* in _____?
- What is the *value* of change in _____?
- What are the *characteristics* of change in _____?
- What are the *characteristics* of _____ that promote change?
- Does change serve a *function/purpose* in _____?

Are students involved in generating key questions for study? Definitely yes! Students should be encouraged to pursue questions that interest them. Generally, teachers craft a set of core questions that frame the unit. Students then supplement this list with questions of their own. There is no magic number of questions. In our experience, we have seen strong units developed around a single key focus question. An example: How does conflict evolve, and how is it resolved? In other cases, more than one key focus question is needed; however, more than eight to ten questions may be too many for students to track. Questions can also be customized to meet the developmental needs of individual students.

Question Answer Relationship Strategy (QAR)

The *QAR* is an effective tool for students to use when sharing what they have learned. However, we include it here as a Prepare tool that the teacher may want to teach up front to students to help them in answering key focus questions. QAR was created Dr. Taffy E. Raphael[18] to assist students to respond to questions traditionally found at the end of textbook chapters.

QAR is built upon a taxonomy of questions. This taxonomy classifies questions according to their relationship to two sources of information that will help the reader answer the question. The two sources of information are the text or the reader's background knowledge. The taxonomy includes three types of questions. They are listed in Figure 2.17.

Textually Explicit:	a) A question whose answer is stated explicitly in the text.
Textually Implicit:	b) A question where the information needed to answer the question is located in several sentences or paragraphs. The reader must integrate this information to generate the answer.
Scriptually Implicit:	c) A question whose answer must be supplied from the reader's background knowledge. The reader needs to activate a schema or script to generate the answer.

Figure 2.17 Three types of questions

To teach students these three different question types, Raphael created four QAR strategies. Figure 2.18 summarizes the four strategies.

Strategy	Definition
Right There (Textually Explicit)	The answer is easy to find in the reading. The words used to make up the question and the words used to answer the question are right there in the same sentence.
Think and Search (Textually Implicit)	The answer to the question is in the reading. The answer is made up of information that comes from more than one sentence or paragraph. You have to put together information from different parts of the reading to find the answer.
The Author and You (Scriptually Implicit)	The answer to the question is not in the reading. Think about what the author tells you and what you already know.
On My Own (Scriptually Implicit)	The answer to the question is not in the reading. You can answer the question without reading the story. You can answer the question by thinking about what you already know.

Figure 2.18 Four QAR strategies

So, craft a set of key focus questions with students. Be explicit with your students who are struggling with the text. Help them identify which questions are "right there" in the text, which are "think and search" questions, which are "the author and you" questions, and which are "on my own" questions.

Enough Already!

In chapter 2, we introduced you to a useful tool to teach the process approach to students: the Prepare, First Dare, Repair, and Share template. In addition, we described a number of generic strategy families tied to this generic four-step process. Finally, we described a number of tools ("cards in our Prepare suit") that we use to help students prepare to take in information. Figure 2.19 summarizes the tools introduced.

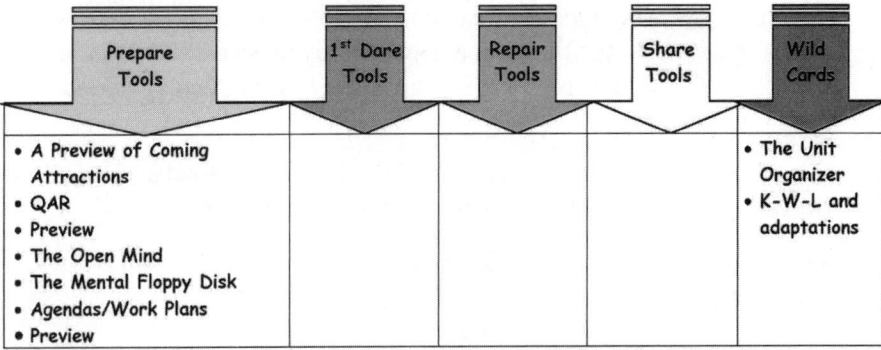

Figure 2.19 Teaching devices introduced in chapter 2

Next we move into First Dare suit teaching tools in chapter 3. But before we do that, take a minute and think about a unit you are currently teaching or planning to teach in the near future. Do any of these tools have applicability to your unit? If so, which tools? Can they be adapted to better meet your student needs?

End Notes

1. Lewin, L., & Shoemaker, B. (1993). Curriculum and assessment: Two sides of the same coin. *Educational Leadership, 50*(8), 55–57.

2. Wright, S. P., Horn, S. P., & Sanders, W. L. (1997). Teacher and classroom context effects on student achievement: Implications for teacher evaluation. *Journal of Personnel Evaluation in Education, 11,* 57–67.

3. Marzano, R. J. (2003). *What works in schools: Translating research into action.* Alexandria, Virginia: Association for Supervision and Curriculum Development, 72–73.

4. Sanders, W. L., & Horn, S. P. (1994). The Tennessee value-added assessment system (TVAAS): Mixed-model methodology in educational assessment. *Journal of Personnel Evaluation in Education, 8,* 299–311.

5. Haycock, K. (1998). Good teaching matters . . . a lot. *Thinking K–16, 3*(2), 1-14.

6. Marzano, R. J. (2003). Ibid. p. 72.

7. Lewin, L., & Shoemaker, B. (1998). *Great performances: Creating classroom-based assessment tasks.* Alexandria, Virginia: Association for Supervision and Curriculum Development.

8. Klingner, J. K., & Vaughn, S. (1999). Promoting reading comprehension, content learning, and English acquisition through collaborative strategic reading (CSR). *The Reading Teacher, 52,* 738–747. The reader is encouraged to read more about CSR in a new book by these authors titled, *From clunk to click,* and published by Sopris West Educational Services in Longmont, Colorado.

9. Lenz, K., Bulgren, J., Schumaker, J., Deshler, D., & Boudah, D. (1994). *The unit organizer routine.* Lawrence, Kansas: Edge Enterprises.

10. Ibid., p. 2.

11. Ibid., p. 2.

12. Lewin, L., & Shoemaker, B. (1998). Ibid.

13. The reader is encouraged to contact the University of Kansas Center for Research on Learning for formal training in the use of the routine and the nine other concept enhancement routines presented in this chapter.

14. Ogle, D. (1986). A teaching model that develops active reading of expository text. *The Reading Teacher, 39,* 564.

15. Adapted from: Tomlinson, C. A. (1999). *The differentiated classroom: Responding to the needs of all learners.* Alexandria, Virginia: The Association for Supervision and Curriculum Development.

16. Naylor, P. R. (1992). *Shiloh.* New York: Macmillan.

17. Kaplan, S. N. (1986). The grid: A model to construct differentiated curriculum for the gifted. In Joseph S. Renzulli (Ed.), *Systems and models for developing programs for the gifted and talented.* Mansfield Center, Connecticut: Creative Learning Press, Inc.

18. Adapted from: Raphael, T. E. (1984). Teaching learners about sources of information for answering comprehension questions. *Journal of Reading, 27,* 303–311.

CHAPTER
THREE

Getting Started: The First Dare Suit

"Deal Me In"

When a player says, "Deal me in," he is saying, "Cards for me, please; I am ready to play cards." Teachers at the First Dare stage want to deal cards to students (use teaching devices) that will encourage all students to want to join in.

Larry's Story

Julius was not convinced. Sure, he had read the short story, "The Challenge."[1] And yes, he had used sticky notes to help track his understanding and appreciation of the fictional work, but he was uncomfortable with the final part of the assignment: to give feedback to the author.

"I don't think I can do this," he declared, when the class was asked if anyone had a question or comment. "Who am I to tell this important guy what I think of his writing? I don't even think I ought to do this."

I knew what he meant. Julius and some others felt presumptuous judging the work of a famous author. The truth was that even though they had strong opinions about the story, they didn't know how to get started on this challenging assignment. Feeling inadequate to the challenge of the task caused their hesitancy.

And I thought I knew what the real problem was: He and his classmates had Prepared for this assignment, due to the careful preparation of their teacher Dorothy Syfert, aided by me, her guest coteacher. But he and some of the others weren't ready for First Dare—that is, to take the plunge into a new, challenging, upper-level thinking assignment: to critique an author by expressing what they liked about the writing, what they didn't like, what confused them, impressed them, or what they could suggest to the author for improvements. The students had never done this type of work, so some of them, like Julius, were uncomfortable with the risk involved.

The First Dare

Why call this stage the First Dare? Because when students are approaching new information, it implies taking a risk. To Prepare for learning, a student must get ready, experiences an anticipatory set, activates existing schemata, and ponders the possibilities. Now our focus shifts to putting all that preparation into motion on an assignment—making a commitment, diving in, taking the plunge. It is critical at this stage to deal your cards (use teaching devices) that will encourage students to join in the game.

For example, the writing process that comes to us from professional authors begins with prewriting (Prepare). Just as the pros do, students brainstorm ideas, perhaps take notes, construct a graphic organizer as a potential framework, interview a source, or go off on the Internet to locate potential Web sites. After all this preparation comes the first draft (First Dare): committing the above thoughts to action. It requires venturing into new territory. Obviously, writers who have Prepared are better able to First Dare.

Likewise, the reading process, which nicely mirrors the writing process, begins with "prereading," strategies for getting your brain in gear by: (a) checking out the text structure or organizational pattern selected by the author, (b) thinking about what you already know about this topic, (c) making a prediction about what you think the author will be teaching you, and (d) asking guided questions. All this gets the reader ready for the main event: a first time, initial reading of the information for comprehension. This takes a commitment to actually do the work. It is a challenge, a risk, your First Dare. How successful students are at this First Dare stage depends upon a number of factors, of course, but three key ingredients to learning new content information are:

- the ability to organize information in meaningful ways;
- the ability to troubleshoot roadblocks that interrupt the construction of meaning of that information; and
- the ability to sort out the key ideas from the supporting details.

Just as with the Prepare stage, the First Dare stage necessitates the possession of a set of strategies available to the learner to be applied at key moments. The more strategies one has mastered, the easier it is to overcome blockages in the learning of new information. Simply put, skilled learners possess far more learning strategies under the hood than do less skilled learners.

And for both skilled and less skilled learners, there are always roadblocks. For example, maybe the author of your textbook is somewhat inconsiderate of your students by not including appropriate boldface subheadings to delineate important subtopics. Or, perhaps the videotape you are showing your class lacks a solid cohesion in its narrative structure. Or, suppose that some of your students lack the ability to visualize key scenes in a literature selection and, therefore, begin to experience comprehension meltdown.

So what are the critical First Dare learning strategies that students can use to prevent these comprehension failures? Consider this list, and ask yourself: "Are these the kinds of abilities that I want my students to master?"

- Focusing
- Info gathering
- Self-regulating
- Generating
- Organizing

(See chapter 2, Figure 2.2, for definitions of these strategies.)

Now, it is one thing to suggest that all students gain proficiency in applying the above First Dare strategies. It is quite another to teach them how to proficiently put them into action.

What follows is a set of classroom learning tools that will assist you in teaching your students how to First Dare core content knowledge more successfully. That is, here are a number of new, different—and maybe even fun—teaching tools that train young learners how to apply strategies that will maximize their understanding of new content information.

My Reading—My Thinking Chart

A very simple First Dare activity is the *My Reading—My Thinking Chart*. A piece of paper is divided into two columns and labeled "My Reading" and "My Thinking/My Thoughts." The first column lists guided questions for the students; the questions are for basic recall of the content information. In column two, "My Thinking," students also get a set of guided questions; but this time, the questions are for deeper processing of the content—that is, interpretation or evaluation.

Here is an example I designed for John Strehl's ninth-grade Integrated Science class for a textbook reading on "Chemical Reactions" (see Figure 3.1).

Notice how the student goes beyond recall of information in column one to a deeper engagement with the content in column two by commenting on the book's example, comparing it to her own examples, her honest understanding of a key concept, and an extension from the book to a real life example.

It is simple to create. All teachers have generated guided questions for their students; these go into column one. Now add deeper processing questions, those that require students to actually *think* about the content, in column two. And what's to stop a teacher from adding a third column, titled "My Evaluation," where students are prompted to critique the author.

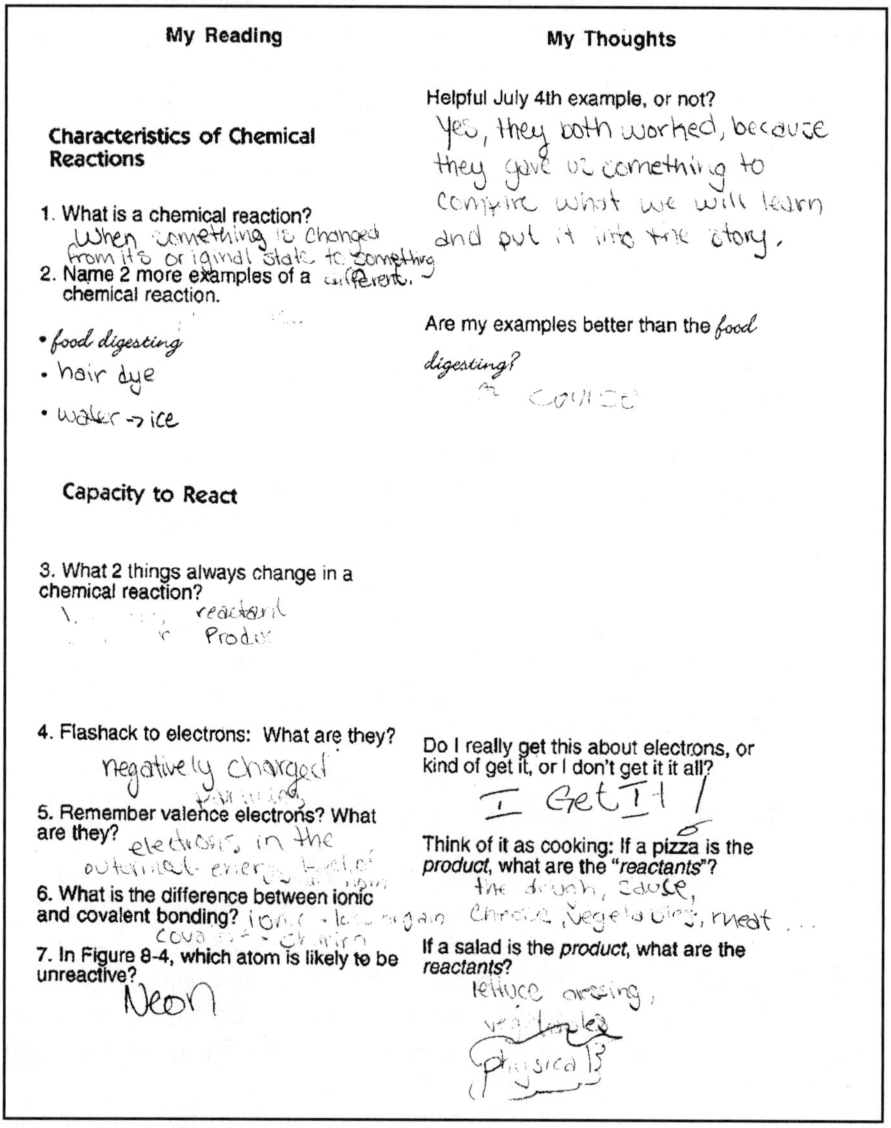

My Reading

Characteristics of Chemical Reactions

1. What is a chemical reaction?
   When something is changed from its original state to something different.
2. Name 2 more examples of a chemical reaction.
   - food digesting
   - hair dye
   - water → ice

Capacity to React

3. What 2 things always change in a chemical reaction?
   1. reactant
   2. product

4. Flashback to electrons: What are they?
   negatively charged

5. Remember valence electrons? What are they? *electrons in the outermost energy level*

6. What is the difference between ionic and covalent bonding? *ionic — losing an e-, covalent — sharing*

7. In Figure 8-4, which atom is likely to be unreactive?
   Neon

My Thoughts

Helpful July 4th example, or not?
Yes, they both worked, because they gave us something to compare what we will learn and put it into the story.

Are my examples better than the *food digesting?*
of course

Do I really get this about electrons, or kind of get it, or I don't get it it all?
I Get It!

Think of it as cooking: If a pizza is the *product*, what are the "*reactants*"?
the dough, sauce, cheese, vegetables, meat

If a salad is the *product*, what are the reactants?
lettuce, dressing, veggies
(physical?)

Figure 3.1 Chemical reactions

Double-Column Entry

This activity mirrors one for a literature First Dare called the *Double-Column Entry,* which we learned from fifth-grade teacher Betty Kasow at Guy Lee Elementary School in Springfield, Oregon. This tool is used for students to respond to either a piece of fiction or nonfiction writing.

Students fold their notebook paper in half vertically (or draw a straight line down the center). The left column is labeled "Statement" (excerpt from the reading) and the right column "My Reaction" (see Figure 3.2).

Students find an excerpt from the text that they feel strongly about. It might create a strong feeling, trigger a memory, click a vivid image, or be written in particularly beautiful language. In a nonfiction piece, the excerpt might be an opinion the student agrees or disagrees with, an important new idea, or a statement they want to further develop. Students copy the excerpt in the left column. In the right column, the students share their reaction to it. Elaborate responses here are encouraged (and modeled).

Excerpt	My Reaction
Copy the **statement** from the text below.	Write your **reaction** to that statement below.

Figure 3.2 Double-columned entry

Several modifications of this Double-Column Entry come to mind. Instead of reading a textbook or literary piece, this tool could be used when viewing a video or filmstrip, or listening to music. Likewise, this tool can easily be adapted for older students by adding a third column and labeling it "Another Student's Reaction." Students would then exchange papers and respond to both the author's statement as well as the first student's reaction. We dub this the *Triple-Column Entry*. It would be especially useful when teaching students to identify multiple points of view.

Through Thick and Thin

Good readers differentiate themselves from less-skilled readers in many ways. One key difference is the ability to keep engaged with the text while reading. Several strategies can be applied to accomplish this, including asking questions. Successful readers constantly ask questions of the author, of the teacher, of themselves, of key characters in fiction; less successful readers do not. So here is an activity that stimulates question-asking. It's called *Through Thick and Thin.*

Students are prompted to interrupt their First Dare reading periodically to pause and ask a question. Two types of questions are required. The first type, *Thin* questions, refers to questions that have an easy, obvious answer to them because the author has provided the answer to the reader.

Why would a teacher want students to ask themselves simple, obvious, already answered questions? A couple of reasons include

1. Confidence building. If students can generate an easy question that they already know the answer to, confidence is built: "I read this assignment, and I understood it enough to answer basic, recall questions. Good for me."
2. Asking basic recall questions also serves as a nice review technique; by asking a question and knowing the answer, the student is reprocessing the content, which is always beneficial.

Frances Transure shared this example from her fourth-grade class in Glide, Oregon. Here is Ashley's set of Thin questions generated while First Dare listening to a children's picture book, *The Frog Prince, Continued,* by Jon Scieszka.[2] Handwriting legibility issues aside, she was tracking the story as she listened (see Figure 3.3).

Asking Thin questions can be done orally with a partner or privately on paper. Teachers could model this ability by doing a few in the *Think Aloud* format.

Next, students are instructed to make up a *Thick* question, that is difficult because the author did not provide an answer in the reading. Or, the Thick question might be one generated by the student because he or she doesn't understand the answer provided by the author in the text.

Why have students generate Thick questions? To take them to a higher level of comprehension. Thick questions require readers to go beyond the text, to go beyond the author's information into new territory. This helps them to

1. realize that not all information on a topic can be addressed by an author, i.e., quite often an author deals only with limited information;
2. gain a critical stance towards the author, i.e., by asking a question that transcends the author, students are critiquing the author for missing information;
3. trigger speculation, i.e., hypothesizing, interpreting, reading between the lines;
4. open the door to further research on the topic; i.e., "If the author didn't provide me with all the information, then perhaps I need to look elsewhere."

Getting Started: The First Dare Suit

Additionally, this activity provides critical information to the teacher about what concepts the student is having difficulty comprehending.

Figure 3.4 is Ashley's set of Thick questions for *The Frog Prince, Continued*. She doesn't know the answers to these questions; she is asking for more information. Good news: She is actively listening and processing. Ashley actually liked using this tool. She wrote a note on the back of her Thick and Thin questions: "This was sooo much fun (espally scinc you made our Math period shorter. . .)."

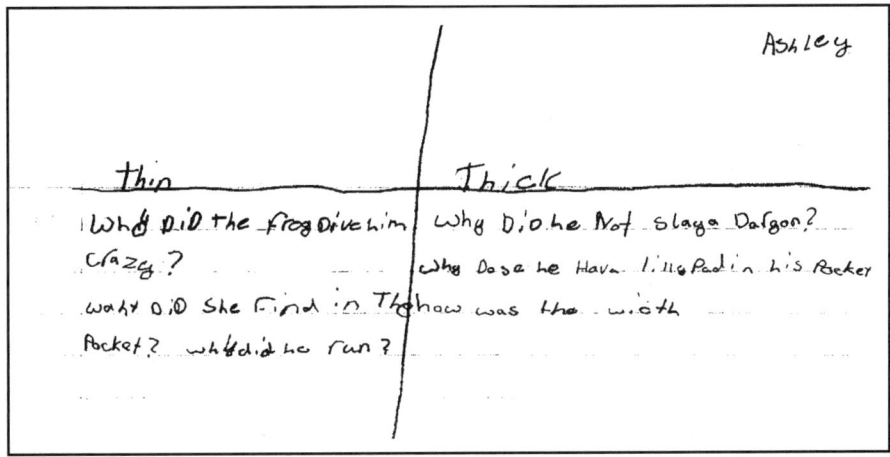

Figure 3.3 Thin   **Figure 3.4** Thick

Thick and Thin questions also work when teaching topics other than literature. Obviously, a student studying science, math, social studies, the arts, or any other subject can generate Thick and Thin questions while reading about the content. To assist them, we can provide this prompt: Thin questions typically begin with Who, What, Where, and When. Thick questions often begin with Why and How.

After students write their Thick and Thin questions, teachers have a number of options for the next step, including:

- asking students to select a Thick and a Thin question and write an answer;
- asking students to meet with a partner, exchange questions, and answer them;
- asking students with partners which Thin questions they have disagreement over the answers to and where they would look to determine the correct answer (back to the text);

- asking students with partners which Thick questions they have disagreement over the answers to and where they would look to determine the correct answer (other possible sources); and
- selecting the best Thick and Thin questions and using them in a quiz or test, giving extra credit to the students who wrote the selected questions.

Teacher Karen Antikajian teaches her third graders that there is actually a third type of question, the *Skinny* question, which is a "yes or no" question. Karen informed her students that *Skinny* questions were taboo—they are too easy to bother with.

SnapShots

SnapShots to Increase Visualization Skills

This technique evolved from a conversation with Chet Skibinski, who taught English Literature at Sunset High School in Beaverton, Oregon. While at a workshop I (Larry) presented on "Assisting Struggling Readers Across the Curriculum," Chet lamented to me that many of his twelfth-grade literature students struggled with comprehending Shakespeare. I speculated that the problem was probably due to vocabulary and grammar issues. Although agreeing that Shakespeare's language is a challenge, Chet thought that his students had difficulty visualizing the action on the stage. Is it not true that many students struggle with the ability of making mental visualizations? We, their teachers, must provide them with assistance in learning how to use this skill.

To increase student visualization ability, a key First Dare strategy, we co-invented the Shakespearean Photo Album, a simple worksheet with empty frames for students to draw quick sketches of what they were picturing as they read a scene. Because not all students possessed fine illustration ability, beneath each frame we added a lined box for students to write a short caption describing the scene (see Figure 3.5).

The *Photo Album* helped Chet teach his students to understand and appreciate classic literature. Not only did it support the key strategy of visualization, it also served to assist student organization of their understanding of literature—the sequencing of plot development.

This activity could be converted into a "miniassessment" performance task, in that the teacher could collect and score it to measure comprehension of a scene in a Shakespeare play. A "minitask" is a classroom-based assessment designed to take a class period or less, and to be scored with a scoring guide (rubric).

Figure 3.5   Shakespearean photo album

SnapShots: The Evolution of an Idea

I decided to take this high school tool to middle school. I was curious about its effect on younger students' visualization and organizational skills, so I offered it to Tom Cantwell, a seventh-grade Language Arts teacher at Cal Young Middle School, Eugene, Oregon.

Earlier in the semester, Tom's students had read in their Lit Anthology book the short story, "Seventh Grade," by Gary Soto. As a big fan of Gary's work, I often use his story "The Challenge," so I suggested to Tom that we assign it to his class with a First Dare activity I dubbed *SnapShots*.

SnapShots is a revision of the Photo Album activity. I introduced it to the middle schoolers by holding up my camera and announcing, "Good readers are able to take pictures of important things as they read."

Semi-impressed, one student in the back row asked, "So are you going to give us each a free camera?"

"No," I replied, looking him in the eye. "You don't need an actual camera. The pictures that a reader takes while reading are *mental snapshots*. They represent what you, the reader, are seeing in your mind's eye."

I continued, "So your 'camera' is really your brain snapping away as you read, based on what the author's words are telling you about the characters, the settings, the problems. Your pictures will be quick sketches that you draw. You don't need a camera, but I will provide you with some 'film.'"

This got their attention. Tom and I then distributed a set of yellow 3 in. x 3 in. sticky notes[3] to each student. Predictably, their response to the sticky notes was favorable.

Whenever I use stickies with students, I get an enthusiastic response. When elementary kids get a set of sticky notes from their teacher, they cry out, "Oh, yes! Sticky notes! This is great! We love school! Life is wonderful!"

When middle school kids receive sticky notes, they typically respond with, "Oh, yes! Sticky notes! This is great. . . ." But they stop quickly, remembering that it is not cool to be excited about anything in school. (But they cannot help getting excited about this activity.)

I've even used stickies with high school students, who respond with a bored look and mild contempt. But I know behind the look what they're privately thinking: "Oh, yeah! Sticky notes. This is different! This will be better than the usual blah-blah!" Plus, sticky notes provide them with some relief: A small space to work in means a shorter amount of work to do.

To facilitate the distribution of the stickies to Tom's seventh graders, before class we precounted a set of six sticky notes and adhered the set to a piece of cardstock paper. But when the students received it, they noticed not only a set of yellow stickies but also some blue and pink.

I explained. "You have three different colors of 'film' because on the State Assessment Test you are assessed on three different reading targets:

1. Your comprehension of both literal and nonliteral (inferential information);

2. Extending understanding beyond the text by making mental connections to other source(s); and

3. Critical analysis of the content—evaluating the author's writing, both the style and the ideas presented."

"These are called traits, but let's call them *targets*: You have three targets to hit on this reading assignment. To help you succeed, use the colored film (sticky notes) to make quick sketches as you read. Use yellow film to sketch Trait 1, your understanding of the story; use blue film to sketch memories from other sources that remind you of something you read in the story; use pink film to critically analyze Gary Soto's writing—that is, what you like, don't like, what confused you, what impressed you, what you think he should have done differently."

Now, this assignment requires students to accomplish quite a bit of thinking. To aim for and hit three reading targets on a short story is not an easy task. Both Tom, their teacher, and I felt that it was worth the attempt. Not only would it help train them to perform on an important state assessment more importantly, it would strengthen their literacy skills.

So, being wise teachers, we modeled to the class how to take a SnapShot of each targeted outcome. The twin challenges Tom and I revealed to the students during the modeling were: (a) keeping the three categories straight in your mind, and (b) deciding which ideas are worth preserving in a SnapShot. The students freely asked questions as they watched the demonstration.

Of course, if shooting for—and hitting—multiple targets is too much for a class of students to accomplish, a smart teacher would introduce SnapShots with only one target to hit. Later, an additional target(s) could be added. We do not want a great teaching tool to backfire and cause student overload and frustration.

Good readers can read carefully and critically because they have strategies at their disposal that facilitate the reading. But not all our students possess these strategies; so we, their teachers, teach them explicitly how to read more strategically. Sticky notes are a mechanism to practice one such First Dare strategy; namely, to visualize what the author is describing in the story. And not just picturing the literal level (that is, characters and events), but also crafting mental pictures that connect to the story, the person who wrote the story, and what that author did successfully or not successfully to tell me, the reader, the story.

To heighten the importance of this SnapShot activity, I provided the students with several Photo Album pages, like the Shakespearean Photo Album in Figure 3.5.

This activity worked very well. All the students were very engrossed in taking mental SnapShots using the three colors of "film." While I figured that this would particularly assist those students who struggle with reading comprehension, it actually helped even the stronger readers to maximize their First Dare reading. Check out two student samples: Figure 3.6 created by a struggling reader, and the other is Figure 3.7 by a more solid reader.

Tom and I decided to convert this activity into a performance assessment task. What is the difference? A task heightens an activity by accompanying it with an explicit scoring device—like a rubric—that informs the student-performer in advance what the targeted objectives (traits) are and how they will be scored (on a 3-point, 4-point, 5-point, or 6-point scale). By presenting the rubric to the students before they begin reading, they know what targets to shoot for; during the reading they can checkin to monitor their own progress. After the task is completed, they then use it to double-check for all required targets. Finally, the teacher-judge uses the rubric to objectively and consistently score the students' work.

Figure 3.6

Figure 3.7

The ChecBric

I actually used a modified rubric, called the *ChecBric*,[4] with this seventh-grade class. A ChecBric is a scoring device Betty and I invented that is a hybrid of a checklist and a rubric. Get it? Chec + Bric = ChecBric. The left column is a checklist for students to examine before beginning the task, during the task, and after completion of the task to double-check for all required targets. The right column is the rubric for the teacher to use to score the individual students' work. Figure 3.8 shows the ChecBric I designed for Tom's class.

What about SnapShots as a reading assistant in another subject besides English and Language Arts? Could a science teacher employ this teaching tool while showing the class a videotape, say, on the life cycle of a monarch butterfly? And could primary students use SnapShots as they listen to their teacher read to them a picture book?

Storyboards

Pam Huling, a teacher at Cal Young Middle School, uses a different visual representation tool: *Storyboards*. Similar to the *comic strip,* a storyboard is a

SnapShots ChecBric

Target 1: I Understand the Reading
___ I identified the author's main ideas
  • characters
  • setting
  • problem
  • ending
___ I commented on the author's key supporting details
___ I've shown that I "read between the lines" to make inferences
  • the theme
___ I offered support by referring back to the story

Trait 1: Demonstrates Comprehension of the Reading

6 = **exceptional** comprehending; thorough and convincing
5 = **excellent** comprehending; strong understanding
4 = **proficient** comprehending; competent, good enough
3 = **inadequate** comprehending; close, but inconsistent, incomplete
2 = **limited** comprehending; confused or inaccurate
1 = **missing** comprehending; NO attempt to meet expectations, OR virtually NO understanding

Target 2: I Connect the Reading to Another Source

Note: You do <u>not</u> need to do all of these, but you must explain <u>why</u> you are making the connection.
___ I've connected the reading to something that happened to me
___ I've connected the reading to something that happened to someone I know
___ I've connected the reading to something that I read
___ I've connected the reading to something that I watched on TV
___ I've connected the reading to a movie or videotape
___ I've connected the reading to some issue or event in my community or the world at large

Trait 2: Extends Understanding Beyond the Reading

6 = **exceptional** connecting; thorough and complex
5 = **excellent** connecting; outstanding and strong
4 = **proficient** connecting; competent, good enough
3 = **inadequate** connecting; scant or inconsistent; fails to explain why and how the source connects to the story
2 = **limited** connecting; superficial or flawed; no explanation
1 = **missing** connecting; NO attempt to meet expectations, OR does NOT show a connection to anything

Target 3: I Read Critically by Giving Feedback to the Author

___ I've identified the author's purpose
___ I've evaluated the author's stylistic devices:
  • structure
  • point of view
  • word choice
___ I've analyzed author's use of literary elements:
  • metaphor/simile
  • symbolism
  • foreshadow/flashback
___ I've supported by critique with relevant evidence from the text
___ I've made reasoned judgments about the author's writing
  • offered praise
  • suggestions to polish
  • asked questions

Trait 3: Reads Critically by Analyzing the Text

6 = **exceptional** analyzing; thorough and convincing
5 = **excellent** analyzing; strong, outstanding
4 = **proficient** analyzing; competent, good enough
3 = **inadequate** analyzing; incomplete
2 = **limited** analyzing; confused or unfounded
1 = **missing** analyzing; NO attempt to meet expectations, OR NO evidence of analysis

Source: Traits are taken from the Oregon Dept. of Education's Reading Informative and Literary Texts Scoring Guide, 1998, Office of Assessment and Evaluation, O.D.E., 255 Capitol St. NE, Salem, OR 97310.

ChecBric ©2001, Larry Lewin Educ.Consulting
541•343•1577 / larry@larrylewin.com

Figure 3.8 SnapShots ChecBric

visual representation of a set of scenes in a story, either a true story like in a news event, a past story from a historical event, or a fictional event from literature. Imitating what some movie directors do to lay out a film's events, students draw pictures for each major action in a scene. Labels can be jotted below to identify key characters' names, settings, and so forth. Pam wisely typed up and distributed directions to her students to ensure their success (see Figure 3.9).

Debbie Haddock, from the North Thurston School District in Lacey, Washington, also employs storyboards. She sent us an outstanding example created

```
                                          Name _____
                                          Date _____

                     Book Report
                  Theme:  War/Conflict
        ----------------------------------------------


   Create a storyboard with 20 frames.
        -Sketch the scene

   Include in the storyboard the following:
        -Introduction
        -Explain the main characters
        -A clear description of the conflict
        -Examples of rising action
        -The conclusion

   *The last five frames: Analyze the situation today.
        -Include your prediction, based on research, how this
            conflict effects the future.


   Title your storyboard.
        List the author.
   This layout may be color-coded.


   Work must be grammatically correct.
   Neatness always counts.
   Present to class.
        Evaluate the author's skill.  What did the author do to
        create interest?   What did the author do well?
        (characterization, building plot, foreshadowing, etc..)
        Did the author use techniques such as descriptive language,
        figurative language, point of view, symbolism, etc. ?
        Thumbs up or down recommendation with supporting reasons.


   Due: _____
```

Source: Pam Huling, Cal Young Middle School, Eugene, OR

Figure 3.9

by eighth grader Christine, as she read and closely tracked Maya Angelou's *I Know Why the Caged Bird Sings*. Not only does this student possess a fine drawing ability that produced a visually pleasing work, more importantly, she nailed the key events in her storyboard (see Figure 3.10).

Getting Started: The First Dare Suit

Figure 3.10

High school students also benefit when their teachers employ visual representation tools in their teaching. Eric Schott teaches English Lit. at Shaler Area High School in Pittsburgh. His students were required to form a team to make an illustration of a key event in *Macbeth,* and to then write a paragraph on the back explaining its importance to the scene (see Figure 3.11).

Figure 3.11

Stick to It

Another use of sticky notes during a First Dare reading is called *Stick to It,* suggested by Paul Weill, former teacher and now a curriculum specialist at the Lane County, Oregon, Educational Service District. Students use color-coded sticky notes to track their comprehension and stick to it to construct meaning. Students are instructed to write comments, references, and questions to highlight important information and to monitor their own construction of meaning. They stick the stickies right on the text they are reading. This teaching tool is especially useful when using textbooks or library materials that cannot be written on.

Kathleen Carson's ninth-grade English Literature class at Glide High School in Glide, Oregon, was assigned to read a translated version of Homer's *The Odyssey*—not an easy read by any means. To support reading comprehension and appreciation of this classical literary piece, each student was given a set of 30 sticky notes, 10 each in 3 different colors with the following designations: (a) blue for a quick summary, a translation into your own words, or a key point to note, (b) green for a question that arises, a tough vocabulary word, or a guess you are making, and (c) pink for the theme—the author's intended message.

Figure 3.12

The class's literature anthology was formatted with a wide right margin for notes, so this is where the students posted their stickies (see Figure 3.12).

Of course, a wise teacher would not assume that all students in the class could do this "sticky reading" by merely listening to the teacher's directions. Rather, it would be smart to model the procedure. So, Kathleen demonstrated to the ninth graders by reading aloud the first section and writing a sticky for each category. As she did this "think aloud" activity, she asked students to offer alternative suggestions for stickies in each color. Thus, the demonstration moved toward releasing them for independent work by removing the scaffolds she had provided for them.

Remember Julius, the concerned student in Dorothy Syfert's class, who was uncomfortable critiquing an author? Before he was assigned the critique, he and his classmates were given a set of colored sticky notes to help track the story reading. They used three different colors for three different aspects of the reading, including green stickies to critically analyze the author's writing style.

Each student recorded three comments on the stickies and stuck them right at the places in the story that triggered the comments. The completed green stickies were then used later to launch the critique of the author.

Stick to It naturally works in other subjects as well. Just tailor the categories for different colored stickies to meet your needs. For example, a science class reading about matter in the textbook could code stickies for the attributes of solids, liquids, or gases.

The Open Mind

Another visual tool, introduced in chapter 2 as a Prepare tool, is the Open Mind. This is a simple, yet hugely effective, teaching tool that can also be used to assist students at the First Dare stage.

The Open Mind is a worksheet with an outline of a human head. Inside the head, each student draws a picture of what he or she is thinking while reading, listening, or viewing in class. This allows the student to jot ideas down in a user-friendly format, a sort of "disguised note taking" activity. The "thoughts" also could be those of a character in a novel or short story, those of a historical figure, or those of anyone the teacher or class decides upon.

Kayla, a student in Doug Vickery's fourth-grade class at Glide Elementary School, tracked her understanding of the award-winning children's book *Click, Clack, Moo*.[5] Instead of drawing pictures inside the Open Mind, she opted for writing the characters' thoughts using a common cartooning tool: thought bubbles (see Figure 3.13).

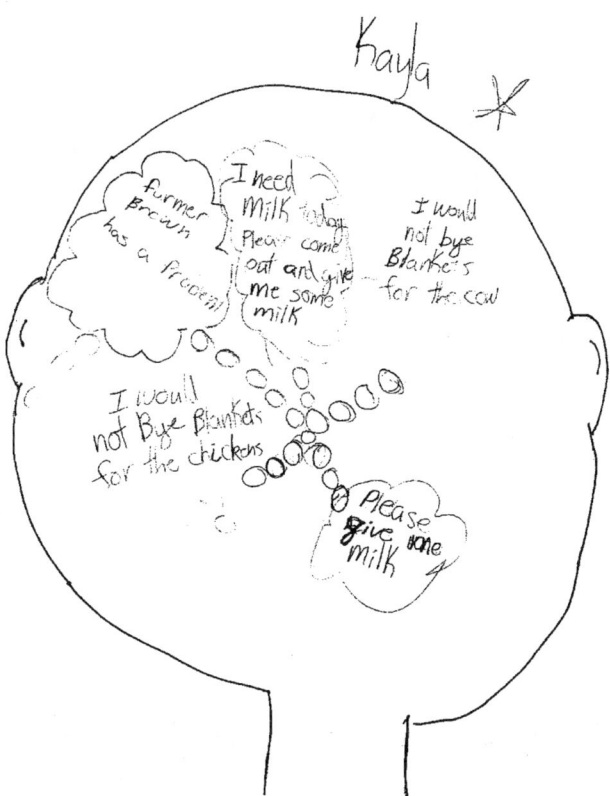

Figure 3.13

Click and Clunk

Click and Clunk is a First Dare tool developed by Janette Klingner and Sharon Vaughn.[6] It is a useful tool for constructing meaning from text. They introduce this teaching tool:

> Click and Clunk is when you think about what you are reading and check to make sure you understand everything. When you find words you don't understand, you figure out what they mean. We say that words or ideas we understand "click." Words or ideas we don't understand "clunk."[7]

Clicks:

- When we understand what we read, everything "clicks" along smoothly.

Clunks:

- When we don't understand what we read, "clunk," we stop.
- When we get to a clunk, we use fix-up strategies to try and figure out what the clunk means, so we can continue onward.

Students are taught the following Clunk Fix-Up Strategies:

- Reread the sentence with the clunk, and look for key ideas to help you figure out the word.
- Think about what makes sense.
- Reread the sentences before and after the clunk, looking for clues.
- Look for a prefix or suffix in the word that might help.
- Break the word apart, and look for smaller words that you know.

Notice that the Click and Clunk tool has moved into "fix-up" strategies, which we call Repair. This nicely demonstrates how this learning process is *recursive* in nature: Learners do not necessarily move straight forward from Prepare to First Dare into Repair finishing with Share. Rather, they move forward *or backward* with each stage as they need to—in order to construct understanding. This forward and backward looping makes the process flexible and more powerful. Click and Clunk employs First Daring and Repairing.

Pocket Organizer

This First Dare strategy helps students organize notes as they conduct research. It is adapted from a "Fact Facts Folder" strategy presented by Kay Law.[8]

On the cover of a manila (or other color) file folder, students record what they think they already know about their research topic (tapping prior knowledge from their schemata) and record a set of questions generated to guide their research (setting a motivating purpose).

Inside the file folder, they paste library book pockets (or small manila envelopes with the flaps cut off). On, or under, each pocket, the student writes one of the guided questions recorded earlier. In each pocket or envelope, students will place index cards on which they have recorded their notes related to that question.

The student also writes a number that relates to the resource used for that information. These resources can be listed on the back of the file folder for the later creation of a bibliography.

In a second column on the back of the file folder, the student records one new thing to teach someone about the topic after each day of researching. Students share this new information daily with a partner or in a group.

For lower-performing students, the teacher could suggest color-coding the pockets and index card with colored markers to assist the categorizing of sub-topics.

The *Pocket Organizer* is a powerful tool for organizing new information as you process it. We all recognize the need for such a tool. Who has experienced the pain of having a student dump a pile of notes, papers, and assignments on our desk asking us for help?

Folded Bookmark

Yvonne Fasold, high school English teacher and assessment coordinator at Sheldon High School, developed the *Folded Bookmark* to help her students maximize their First Dare readings with painless note taking.

Students take a piece of white notebook paper, turn it landscape (sideways), fold it in half, and then in half again.

They open the paper and number each column as 1, 2, 3, and 4 on the front, and then turn the paper over and label the columns 5, 6, 7, and 8 on the back. The teacher provides a prompt for each number, so that the students respond to the reading in a number of different ways.

As the students read an assignment (a textbook, a novel, an article), they record their responses in the columns. Between readings, the Folded Bookmark is placed into the text serving as a bookmark.

Yvonne suggests using this Folded Bookmark in a number of ways:

1. Students use it as a running record for note taking. They should be instructed as to where in the reading notes should be taken from, how often a note needs to be taken, and in which column it should be recorded.

2. Instead of using student notebook paper, the teacher could create a template with a prompt typed in each column. Guided prompts can be

tightly or loosely structured to trigger responses to theme, character development, vocabulary acquisition, quotations, etc.

3. Younger learners can copy words or phrases or make illustrations in the columns as they read instead of responding to teacher prompts.
4. Obviously, this tool can easily be adapted to a listening or viewing assignment.

Graphic Organizers (GOs)

Graphic Organizers (GOs), sometimes called concept webs, mental maps, or idea clusters, have been a popular teaching tool in many classrooms over the past two decades. We would be remiss not to include them in this chapter on First Dare.

Remember, during a First Dare, students need to use strategies to focus on what is important, to self-regulate their construction of meaning, and to organize the new information. SnapShots and other visual tools can help them do this.

And so can a Graphic Organizer, which is an excellent device for students to track and arrange their learning. They work well at all grade levels and for all subjects, because they offer students an organizational pattern to park newly constructed content information as well as show the relationships of that information.

For example, here is a fifth-grade literature example from Linda Barber, of Guy Lee Elementary School in Springfield, Oregon, for the short story "*Eleven*," by Sandra Ciscernos.[9] Linda knew that her students would benefit from a set of guided questions to help track their understanding of the story's plot. But she also knew that a set of questions is often a turn-off to students, so she repackaged them into a more user-friendly format, the Graphic Organizer. Notice that she encouraged the class to employ visualization by drawing a picture of the most important scene in the middle bubble of the GO (see Figure 3.14).

Graphic Organizers allow learners to use their visual, spatial, and global mental powers to process and organize construction of meaning. They are very similar to the good old outline, a teaching tool that has a centuries-long track record. Outlines do what graphic organizers do, but they work in a more linear, sequential format.

Which approach is best for kids? Obviously, that answer depends on the kid. Some of our students work best in one mode, and others are comfortable using another mode. So why not teach them both outlining and graphic organizing, so they can work comfortably in both formats.

A smart way of teaching both is to incorporate computer technology into our instruction by using Inspiration® software.[10] This software program allows students to construct electronic graphic organizers (*EGOs*) on a computer. Many

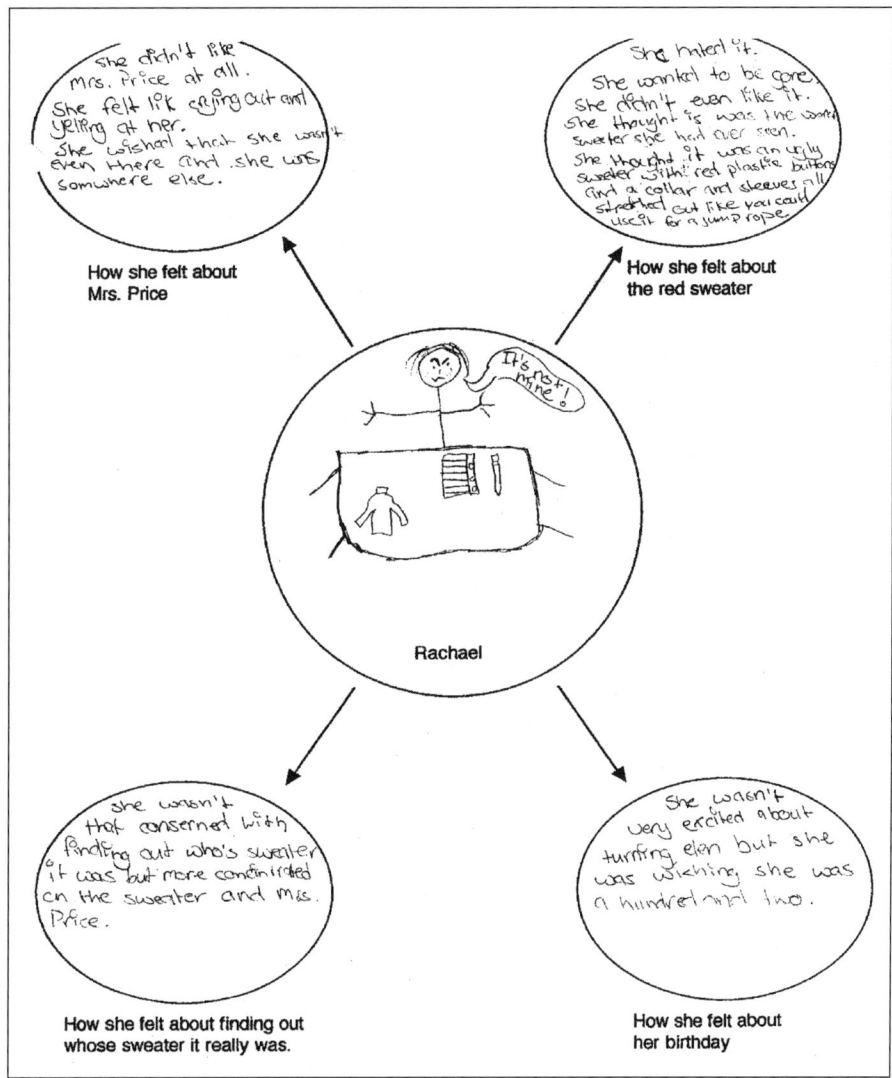

Figure 3.14

teachers have created GOs using the draw features of our word processing program. However, Inspiration® is designed to streamline and enhance this. What are some of the benefits of using Inspiration®?

- A library of over 1000 shapes, symbols, and icons to choose from
- The connecting arrows automatically link the shapes
- Lots of color choices
- Built-in spell checker
- Optional use of electronic sticky notes

- Ease of editing, moving, making changes
- A set of 24 ready-made EGO templates
- One-click transformation from EGO to outline

That's right: After a student creates an *electronic graphic organizer* on the computer with Inspiration®, one mouse click converts it into an outline. The software also allows a student to begin with an outline and then convert it into the diagram mode (Graphic Organizer, see Figure 3.15). Primary teachers, check out the new Kidspiration designed specifically for K–3 students.[10]

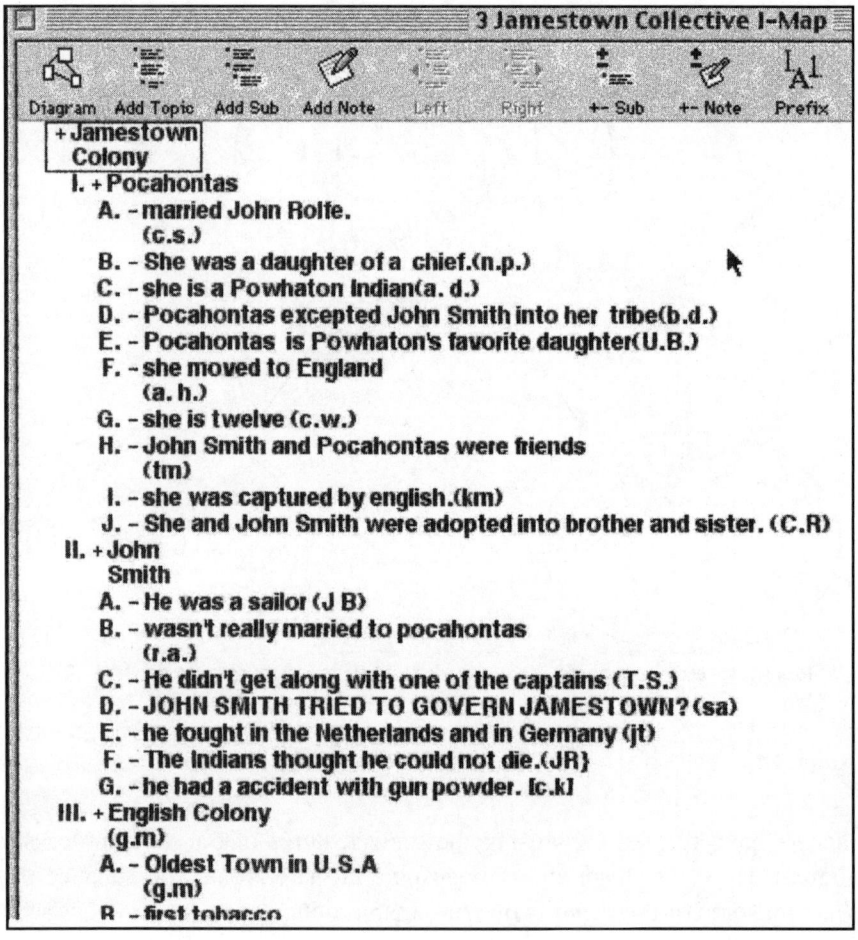

Figure 3.15 Outline format in Inspiration® software

Get the Gist

This First Dare tool also comes from Collaborative Strategic Reading (CRS).[11] To *Get the Gist* of a reading assignment, a student will:

1. name the *who* or *what* a paragraph or section was mostly about.
2. tell the most important thing about the *who* or *what.*
3. say the gist in 10 words or less.
4. write the gist in a Learning Log (individual student journal, see Figure 2.7).

When learning this tool, students can work with a partner, a small group, or the entire class.[12]

Theory Stop: The Importance of Constructing Meaning "From the Get Go"

Let's take a minute and reflect on the tools introduced in this chapter in light of some very practical research on effective teaching and learning. Dr. Judith A. Langer, director of the National Research Center on English Learning & Achievement at the University at Albany, State University of New York, and a team of researchers have been investigating English/Language Arts programs in two sets of middle and high schools with similar student populations. They worked in 44 classrooms in 25 schools in 4 states.

> In one set of schools, students "beat the odds" and outperform their peers on high-stakes, standardized tests of English skills and read and write at high levels of proficiency. In the other set of schools, students perform more typically. Most of the schools in the study serve students from high-poverty, big-city neighborhoods. By comparing these two sets of classrooms, we have been able to identify and validate six features of instruction that make a difference in student performance.[13]

They identified six features present in the classroom that contributed to higher achievement. We think they have application across the curriculum as well. They are

1. *Students learn skills and knowledge in multiple lesson types.* That means teachers use different teaching devices in the delivery of lessons based on student need. This chapter has introduced you to multiple teaching tools to expedite construction of meaning in the First Dare step.

2. *Teachers integrate test preparation into instruction.* Both teachers and students understand the traits of good performance, and students also understand the purposes for and the requirements of assessments. It is critical that this is accomplished early on in the unit—during the Prepare and First Dare steps. Test preparation is integrated into the class time, as part of the ongoing learning goals. Just to note: We think that using a ChecBric with students is a perfect way to do this. (See page 40.)

3. *Teachers make connections across instruction, curriculum, and life.* Connections are woven throughout lessons, making associations among knowledge, skills, and ideas. Teachers also consistently make references to both in-school and out-of-school applications.

4. *Students learn strategies for doing the work.* Bingo! This book is all about this key research. Students must be explicitly taught strategies for thinking as well as doing—for planning, organizing, completing, or reflecting on the content or activity.

5. *Students are expected to be generative thinkers.* All good teachers move beyond immediate goals (i.e., getting through the lessons in the time allotted) toward deeper understandings that encourage the generation of new and significant ideas. To be generative, students must be engaged. The tools described here assist you to get students engaged "from the get go" and keep them engaged throughout the lesson.

6. *Classrooms foster cognitive collaboration.* Developing both content and skills are treated as social activity. "Minds bump against minds as students interact as both problem generators and problem solvers."[14] As a result, students make creative and critical uses of their knowledge and skills. This is nothing new. For years, teachers have understood the value of cooperative learning in providing scaffolding (peer academic support) for *all* learners.

In summary, Langer states, "It is important to understand that the six features identified in this research are interrelated and supportive of one another. The higher performing schools exhibit all six characteristics. . . . Although addressing one feature may bring about improved student performance, it is the integration of all the features that will effect the most improvement."[15]

In the tools introduced in this chapter, can you see elements of these features? How might these teaching devices described above assist you in implementing them in your classroom?

Conclusion

In chapter 2, we introduced a collection of Prepare tools. In this chapter, we shared a set of First Dare tools (see Figure 3.16).

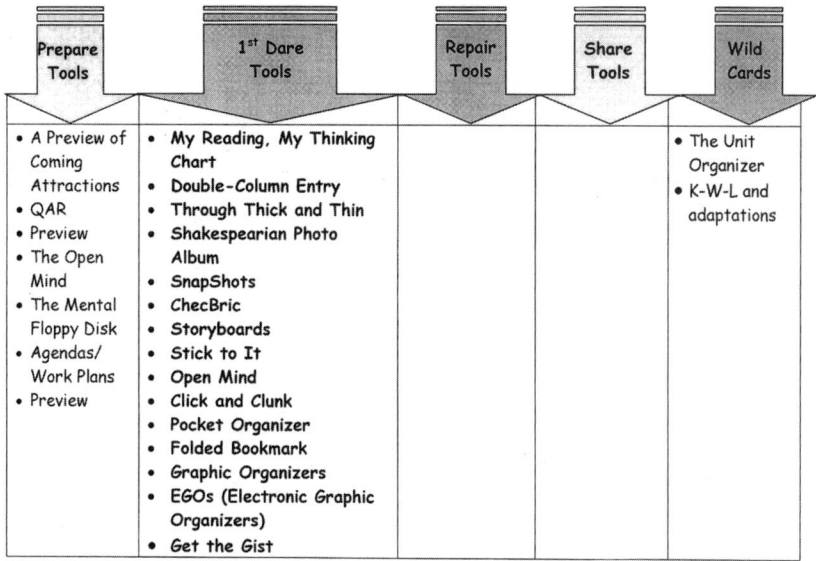

Figure 3.16 Teaching devices introduced in chapter 3

Why the need for these tools? Most students need some help during the learning of new information to incorporate it into their existing schema, to construct meaning from the material, and to organize it in a meaningful way. When they approach new content—whether an elementary student during literature time, a middle schooler in a history class, or a high school student in her math period—this First Dare stage of learning is critical. As teachers, it is our job to provide that help in varying ways. This chapter has presented a set of teaching tools particularly useful for First Daring. These tools vary in their mode, difficulty, and time allocation, but they surely share one purpose: to facilitate the acquisition of content knowledge by providing training in key strategies that maximize understanding.

End Notes

1. Soto, G. (1993). The challenge. *Local news: A collection of stories.* New York: Scholastic, Inc.

2. Scieszka, J. (1994). *The frog prince, continued.* New York: Penguin Putnam Books for Young Readers.

3. "Sticky notes" is the generic term for Post Its®. Other companies manufacture this product, so we will use the term "sticky notes" or "stickies."

4. Lewin, L., & Shoemaker, B. (1998). *Great performances: Creating classroom-based assessment tasks.* Alexandria, Virginia: Association for Supervision and Curriculum Development, p. 34, p. 135.

5. Cronin, D. (2000). *Click, clack, moo.* New York: Simon & Schuster.

6. Adapted from: Klingner, J. K., & Vaughn, S. (1999). Promoting reading comprehension, content learning, and English acquisition through Collaborative Strategic Reading (CSR). *The Reading Teacher, 52,* 738–747. See also citation below for *From clunk to click, Collaborative strategic reading* by Klingner.

7. Klingner, J. K., Vaughn, S., Dimino, J., Schumm, J. S., and Bryant, D. (2001). *From clunk to click, Collaborative strategic reading.* Longmont, Colorado: Sopris West, 2001.

8. Kay Law, Bureau of Education & Research, Bellevue, WA.

9. Ciscernos, S. (1991). Eleven, in *Woman hollering creek and other stories.* New York: Vintage Contemporaries.

10. Inspiration Software, Inc. *Inspiration.* Beaverton, Oregon: Inspiration Software, Inc. Beaverton Hillsdale Hwy., Suite 102, Portland, OR 97225, 800-877-4292, http://www.inspiration.com.

11. Klingner, J. K., Vaughn, S., Dimino, J., Schumm, and Bryant, (2001). *From clunk to click, Collaborative strategic reading.* Longmont, Colorado: Sopris West, 2001.

12. Ibid.

13. The results of this research are reported in a set of research reports and case studies including, *Beating the odds: Teaching middle and high school students to read and write well. Excellence in english in middle and high school: How teachers' professional lives support student achievement,* examines the professional contexts that contribute to teachers' success. A summary of this work can be found on CELA's Web site http://cela.albany.edu (n.d.).

14. Close, E., Angelis, J., & Preller, P. (2001). *Guidelines for teaching middle and high school students to read and write well: Six features of effective instruction.* University at Albany, State University of New York: National Research Center on English Learning and Achievement, p. 14.

15. Ibid., p. 3.

CHAPTER
FOUR

The Repair Suit

"Playing It Close to the Chest, Holding One's Cards Close to the Vest"

In playing cards, this literally means to hold one's cards close to the chest, so no one can see them. In teaching, however, we need to encourage students not to hold their cards close to their chests. We want to know what they are thinking—how they are constructing meaning around our teaching.

Betty's Story

A few years ago, I was chatting with my friend, Bridgette Horn. Bridgette teaches an integrated language arts and social studies seventh-grade block class in a neighboring school district. We were discussing the challenges of addressing students' misconceptions—especially after we have provided what we perceived to be excellent instruction. Bridgette shared this story.

> In a unit on the civil rights movement, I taught a number of lessons on various aspects of the movement, including discrimination in housing, employment, and education. I stressed the importance

of several key court decisions and the passage of laws that attempted to put an end to segregation and discrimination. In particular, we studied major efforts at the federal level to outlaw literacy tests and poll taxes as prerequisites to voter registration. To highlight the difficulties that many African-Americans had in acquiring the right to vote, I shared a film containing a clip from a news broadcast from the early 1960s, showing a number of people attempting to register to vote. Photos graphically illustrated a number of African-Americans being pummeled with water from fire hoses in Birmingham, Alabama. It was clear that the local law enforcement authorities had ordered the dousing. The force of the water pinned many to trees and walls or knocked them down violently.

Toward the end of the unit, I asked students if they had any questions. One young man raised his hand and asked, "I don't understand this. Why do you have to be wet to vote?" I seriously considered early retirement at that moment.

The Challenge of Addressing Misconceptions in the Classroom

We are confident that teachers with any degree of experience in the classroom can relate to this story. Many of us have confronted the challenges of identifying each student's conceptions of the content being taught and then changing, or extending and refining, these conceptions. In this chapter, we will explore tools that teachers might use to do just that—our Repair suit. These tools are designed to get students to take their cards away from their chests and to lay them on the table for us to see.

In chapter 2, we shared a list of strategy families tied to each step in the process. Our goal in this chapter will be to introduce you to teaching tools that can assist your students to use fix-up strategies, evaluating strategies, analyzing strategies, and perspective-taking strategies. Figure 4.1 summarizes the list of strategy families tied to the Repair suit.

But first, we need to spend some time addressing the difference between declarative, procedural, and conditional knowledge, and how one might deal with misconceptions in these three different types of knowledge.

Fixing-up:	Used to resolve any cognitive dissonance
Evaluating:	Used to assess the value, quality, or significance of ideas
Analyzing:	Used to examine essential features as parts of the whole
Perspective Taking:	Used to examine other points of view

Figure 4.1 Repair strategy families

Theory Stop: Different Types of Knowledge

You may have read that knowledge is generally categorized into three distinct types: procedural knowledge, declarative knowledge, and conditional knowledge.[1] (Some refer to conditional knowledge as contextual knowledge.) Let's understand each type so that we can sharpen our pedagogy.

Procedural knowledge is "how to" knowledge—how to read, how to write, how to do basic mathematical algorithms. All of the processes we teach in school—from kindergarten teachers teaching students how to tie their shoes to calculus teachers teaching students to complete a complex algebraic equation—are procedural knowledge. Procedural knowledge involves steps that are usually done in a particular order—a *process*.

Declarative knowledge, as opposed to procedural knowledge, involves the understanding of key ideas. These key ideas are usually organized around subject disciplines and include basic facts, concepts, and generalizations important to that subject discipline. We sometimes refer to this kind of knowledge as "core content knowledge." Science teachers have particular core content they teach; so do math teachers, English teachers, and arts teachers. We all teach content knowledge.

The third type of knowledge, *conditional or contextual,* is not simply procedural or declarative. Conditional knowledge involves drawing from both declarative and procedural knowledge to create something or solve something. Another way to understand conditional knowledge is to see it as metacognition—that is, *thinking* about what you know and what you can do, and drawing from that knowledge in the service of some goal. Figure 4.2 describes these different types of knowledge.

Procedural Knowledge	Declarative Knowledge	Conditional/Contextual Knowledge
Speaking persuasively	Pollution and environmental degradation	Delivering an effective speech on behalf of environmental preservation to the state legislature
Playing the saxophone	Characteristics of various forms of jazz	Performing various jazz classics in a jazz combo
Reading maps	Map legend, latitude, and longitude	Reading a map to plan directions to a specific destination
Problem solving	Electrical circuitry	Restoring power in one's kitchen after the electricity goes off in that room

Figure 4.2 Three different types of knowledge

It is important to understand that teaching students procedural knowledge and teaching them declarative knowledge requires the use of totally different teaching tools. And working with students to Repair both kinds of knowledge, due to incomplete construction of meaning during the First Dare stage, requires the provision of different supports. It is also interesting to note how challenging it is to teach students the use of conditional knowledge. Many of us have discovered that some students seem to acquire both adequate procedural knowledge and declarative knowledge but have great difficulty in using both effectively in various contexts. We all know the frustration, like our science teaching colleagues, of observing students recite basic concepts and pass the quizzes in class on electrical circuitry and then move into the lab and have no clue how to construct a working circuit.

Teaching and Repairing Procedural Knowledge

Let's review how to teach and assist students to Repair their use of procedural knowledge. Then we will follow with a brief discussion of how one teaches declarative knowledge. The bulk of this chapter will include a number of tools to help you work with students to refine and extend their understanding of declarative knowledge.

You may be asking, How does one teach procedural knowledge? It's as simple as one, two, three: model, shape, and make it routine. In step one, the teacher models the steps in the process and uses think-aloud strategies (the teacher makes overt his or her thinking while modeling the process)[2] to demonstrate these steps and the skills involved in each. In step two, students practice each step with guidance and coaching from the teacher. At this stage, the teacher actively points out common errors and pitfalls. In step three, students are given plenty of opportunity to use the process to internalize the application of particular skills and strategies to make them routine. Let's look at the efforts a teacher might make to assist students to Repair their use of procedural knowledge. Figure 4.3 summarizes how this might occur.

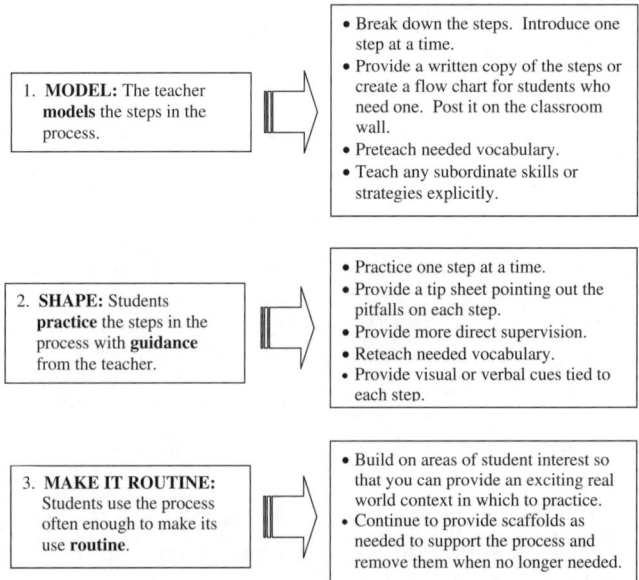

Figure 4.3 Assisting students to **repair** their procedural knowledge

Teaching and Repairing Declarative Knowledge

When teaching declarative knowledge teachers use different steps, including:

1. Use tools to tap prior knowledge.
2. Provide direct and indirect experiences.
3. Provide tools to organize information.
4. Use tools to help students refine their understandings.
5. Provide tools to enhance the storage of the information.

We know from the research literature that what one already knows about the subject to be studied is critical to learning new information.[3] Therefore, an important first step in teaching declarative knowledge involves getting students to tap their prior knowledge and reveal it to the teacher. This thinking typically contains factual information as well as being riddled with misconceptions. We often suggest that teachers say to students, "Instead of a mere penny for your thoughts, a $20 gold piece for your thoughts. That is how important your current thinking is!"

We also know from the research literature that meaning is constructed through direct experiences as well as indirect experiences.[4] Direct experiences include experiencing something firsthand, or simulating the experience. We need to remind ourselves as teachers, "The best thing is *being* there. The next best thing is *simulating* being there." Students may best understand the concepts of personal finance after simulating the management of a family budget. In another example, schools have had great success in helping young teenagers understand the overwhelming responsibilities of parenthood by having them be responsible for a sophisticated doll programmed to behave as an infant. There are a number of excellent resources in the market to provide simulations for use in schools.[5]

Betty likes to share this story of a simulation she conducted in her classroom.

> A number of years ago, I taught a unit on crime lab chemistry to a group of fourth- and fifth-grade students. My colleagues and I taught students several simple procedures, including how to take a fingerprint and how to mount a slide, among others. One task involved the process of thin layer chromatography—that is, having students separate out the substances that make up a mixture. We had a local law enforcement officer come in and ask the class for assistance in identifying which black pen was used to write a ransom note. Small groups were given a piece of the ransom note and six water-soluble pens. It just so happened that we (the teachers) had written the note with a specific brand of overhead marker. After the small groups identified the source pen, one student came over to me and expressed with a great deal of agitation, "This is

awful! A teacher did it. A teacher wrote the ransom note!" I asked how he could be sure that a teacher had done it. He stated emphatically, "A teacher did it all right! They are the only ones who use these kinds of pens." The simulation was all too real for this student.

Indirect experiences include viewing a video or demonstration, reading materials in print or online, or listening to a lecture or explanation. These experiences can also be effective in acquiring core content knowledge. We encourage teachers to provide as many experiences using all senses as possible.

Another key feature of acquiring declarative knowledge is organizing the information in a meaningful way so that it can be worked with—that is, so that it can be compared to and integrated with existing knowledge. And hopefully, the knowledge can then be extended and refined. Teachers must provide students with tools to organize the information meaningfully. These include teaching students to take notes, to create physical and pictographic representations, and to make outlines and graphic organizers, graphs, and charts.

Once knowledge is presented through direct and indirect experiences and is organized so that it can be compared and analyzed with existing understandings, it must then be shaped to resolve any cognitive dissonance that has been created in the process. This shaping and refining is such a challenge when class sizes are growing and state-mandated assessments take so much time away from instruction. At this stage, it is critical to foster a positive and open classroom environment and substantive dialogue both among students and between students and the teacher. Carving out the time to guarantee that this happens is a challenge, but also a must.

The last step in acquiring declarative knowledge is to store this core knowledge in the brain's memory file cabinets. The brain does not easily store information that does not make sense or does not have meaning. (We can all remember the lengths we went to in college to use acronyms and other mnemonic devices in order to cram for tests in classes where the core knowledge presented made no sense and had little meaning.) The more sense it makes and the more meaning it has, the more likely it will be stored. Having students actively engaged in experiencing the core content knowledge will increase the likelihood of the information being stored.

Now Back to the Repair Tools

In exploring how to make instructional interventions with students who persist in holding certain conceptions, one needs to examine why. Figure 4.4 summarizes some typical reasons.

Inconsiderate source materials	The source materials used to introduce students to basic concepts are of such poor quality that they inhibit the construction of meaning.
Student belief systems	Students have deeply held personal belief systems or socio-cultural beliefs that conflict with concepts being taught.
Student naiveté	Students have so few life experiences in general or limited life experiences with this particular phenomena.
Inadequate student vocabulary	Students lack the needed working vocabulary in this discipline to construct meaning from the demonstration, reading, or lecture.
Student locus of attention is elsewhere	Student's attention is focused on meeting other, more pressing needs.
Faulty teaching	The literature has documented numerous cases in which teachers lack the conceptual understanding themselves and as a result teach misconceptions explicitly to students.

Figure 4.4 Reasons why some students persist in holding misconceptions

It is important to attend to these reasons when designing Repair interventions.

When Inconsiderate Text Is the Issue

What do we mean when we say "inconsiderate text"? Inconsiderate text is text that is structured in such a way as to inhibit the construction of meaning by the reader. Quite a bit of research has been done to determine the relationship between text organization and comprehension. Jean Ciborowski in her book, *Textbooks and the Students Who Can't Read Them,*[6] identifies three critical ways in which the textbook itself can inhibit or enhance the construction of meaning by students. They are

- *Structure:* Structure refers to the textbook features that have to do with words, phrases, and sentences, which help cue the reader to upcoming information. Explicit structures, such as headings and subheadings, topic sentences, and clearly written chapter previews, enhance comprehension.

- *Coherence:* Coherence refers to how well ideas are integrated and flow within textbook lessons and across chapters and units. When statements are explicit about the relationship of ideas, when the pronoun references are clearly linked to the nouns they represent, when the graphics illuminate the text, coherence is present and comprehension increases. Many currently published textbooks, when analyzed, have very different writing styles from chapter to chapter (which are often written by different authors); and publishers frequently change the text to accommodate a particular readability formula, which makes it difficult for ideas to flow from one to the next.

- *Audience Appropriateness:* Audience appropriateness has to do with the match between the text and the reader's level of knowledge and reading skill. If the text is too difficult and includes vocabulary that is above the students' level, they are not reading well and cannot comprehend the text. When the text is audience-appropriate, it conveys concepts in such a way that the reader is engaged with the concepts.

To help teachers evaluate the appropriateness of print materials, we encourage them to use a tool we developed called the *UFT Checklist*. The UFT, (*User Friendly Text Checklist*), asks teachers to examine the text in relation to certain criteria (see Figure 4.5).

Ideally, teachers want to select text that scores in the 3 and 4 range on these traits. The higher the score, the more the text has UFT traits. The more the text has UFT traits, the more likely the student will be able to work independently to construct meaning.

User Friendly Text Checklist

More and more educators are acknowledging that many textbooks are written and formatted in such a way that make it difficult for students—particularly lower-performing students—to construct meaning around the content included in the text. Some texts are simply more "considerate" to the learner than others. To help teachers identify which texts might be a better match for students we have identified a number of traits that are present in user friendly text—U F T for short. Use the following checklist to evaluate the printed materials you use with your students.

Text _____   Pages Analyzed _____

Use the following scale:
1   This trait is not present in the text.
2   This trait is present but weak in the text.
3   This trait is present and adequate in the text.
4   This trait is present and strong in the text.

Vocabulary: The text...	1	2	3	4
1. Sets off important vocabulary words critical to understanding the text in boldface or color print?				
2. Provides a pronunciation key for important vocabulary words?				
3. Explicitly teaches the word and the concept it refers to in the text?				
4. Provides an easy-to-use glossary?				

Figure 4.5   The user friendly text checklist

Text Structure and Concept Development: The text...	1	2	3	4
1. Includes a table of contents or outline of key points?				
2. Includes an introduction to the topic stating key chapter or unit concepts clearly?				
3. Includes a summary of key points at the end of the section, chapter, or unit?				
4. As appropriate, includes headings and subheadings to cue the reader as to the main ideas and structure of the passage?				
5. Includes subheadings that relate directly to the main headings?				
6. Uses colors, shapes, font styles, and placement of headings to distinguish between main and subheadings?				
7. Includes a title that reflects the main idea of the chapter or section?				
8. Includes key questions that focus on a balance of factual details, major concepts and critical thinking?				

Graphics: The text...	1	2	3	4
1. Includes illustrations, charts, and graphs that enhance the most important information in the text?				
2. Includes illustrations, charts, and graphs that break up the text to make it more accessible to struggling readers?				
3. Includes charts and graphs that share key information in a clear and concise format?				
4. Includes easy to read legends to interpret data in charts and graphs?				

Figure 4.5 The user friendly text checklist (*Continued*)

When SocioCultural and/or Personal Beliefs Are Deeply Held

At times, students come to school with deeply held values or beliefs that are at odds with the content being taught. This has been particularly true in health and the sciences. As a result, some teachers simply stay away from certain curriculum areas in order to avoid the flak. It is our position that attempting to force any student to give up a deeply held belief is clearly inappropriate. It is important, however, to assist the student in identifying both alternate points of view and those areas in which there is common community consensus.

One tool that you can use to help students sort out the difference between their beliefs and the beliefs of others is by using a tool we adapted from the FLASH curriculum.[7] We call this tool the *Values Response Protocol*.

The Values Response Protocol

In the classroom, statements or questions will arise in the context of some units where the statement or question is clearly related to deeply held beliefs. When that occurs, the FLASH curriculum suggests the following protocol. Let's use the example here of a sixth-grade student asking in class, "How old should a person be to have a baby?"

1. Affirm the statement maker or asker.
   - That's an interesting statement/question.
   - I'm glad you raised that point/asked that question.
   - The point you are making is important to note.
2. Identify the statement or question as a belief statement/question.
   - That's the type of question (or statement) that involves people's beliefs.
3. If there is a factual component to the statement or question, express it or answer it.
   - You asked how old a person should be to have a baby. Let's look at the facts. We know that the healthiest age, for both mother and baby, is in the 20s and the early 30s.
4. Help the class describe the range of beliefs about the topic. Encourage the class to share various points of view. You may have to add some points of view that the class does not raise.
   - Different people believe different things about when a person is ready to become a parent. What do you think some people believe?
5. State a commonly held belief if there is one that is relatively universally held.[8]
   - Most people in our community/nation believe that it is not a good idea to have a baby at your age . . . 12 or 13 years old.
6. If there is no universally held belief about the subject, refer back to the list you generated as a class.
   - Different people believe different things about this topic.

7. Refer students to parents, clergy, and other trusted adults. Also, with older students, encourage them to read some seminal materials on the subject.
    - Check with your parents tonight. Find out what your folks believe about that. Find out what your church or synagogue, temple or mosque teaches, if you belong to one.

OPV: Other Points of View

Another valuable tool that can be used to help students identify other points of view is called *OPV.* OPV is one thinking tool from the CoRT thinking skills program.[9]

Edward DeBono, a physician in Great Britain, developed the CoRT Thinking Program.[10] It is published under the auspices of DeBono's corporation, the Cognitive Resources Trust; thus the name CoRT. The entire CoRT Program has six levels. Each level has several specific thinking tools that are taught in one-to-two week intervals to students in Grades 1 through postsecondary education. In our experience, these tools are highly effective when used by school staffs as well as students in thinking creatively, critically, and in solving problems. The 10 tools taught in *CoRT 1: Breadth* are taught to all students of all ages, regardless of their age or ability. These tools are basic to all thinking activities, according to DeBono. Once these tools are mastered, teachers can then introduce additional CoRT Thinking Program levels. DeBono states that the purpose of the CoRT 1 lessons is to broaden perception so that in any thinking situation we can see beyond the obvious, immediate, and egocentric.

Using OPV, one focuses on seeing things from another's point of view. Students need to be taught that just as they think about the issue/concept/situation, other people also think about them. These other people may have a very different viewpoint. One critical skill in thinking is to be able to tell how other people are thinking about something. If someone really understands another point of view, he or she is able to articulate the differences and similarities between viewpoints. Another point that DeBono makes is that every point of view may be right for the person holding it but not absolute enough to be imposed on others. The reader is encouraged to become familiar with the CoRT Thinking Skills Program, an excellent resource for teaching thinking.

DeBono identifies a particular protocol to use in working with students. This protocol involves teaching the tool separately and then practicing with several issues in small groups. In this case, we suggest that once the tool is learned, students would then be asked to identify the various stakeholders in a particular situation and then work in small groups to generate a position statement from the point of view of each stakeholder. Following the position statement, the small group is then asked to list any rationale in support of that point of view. Each group shares their position statement and rationale with classmates.

Others, including the teacher, then have an opportunity to react and enhance each position. Using the previous example of how old a person should be to have a baby would work here.

OPV can be used with a number of issues, including many initiated by students. Figure 4.6 provides an example of teaching **OPV** with a third-grade class. The issue being discussed was a petition brought to the principal requesting a change in school policy about using skateboards on campus.

The **principal does not want** skateboarding at school because:
- She is worried that kids might get hurt.
- She doesn't want to have kids coming to school early or staying late.
- She thinks that big kids will start hanging around school and causing trouble.
- She is afraid that some older kids will run over little kids.

The **girls** aren't sure if they want skateboarding or not.
- Some girls think that it would be a good idea and some girls don't.
- Some girls think that the boys will chase them on skateboards.
- Some girls think that if the boys are busy with skateboards, they can use the soccer field more.
- Some girls don't care.

Some parents **want** skateboarding because:
- They think it is good exercise and fun.
- It won't hurt anyone.
- It will give kids more things to do.
- There will less trouble on the playground.

Some parents **don't want** skateboarding because:
- They think it is not safe.
- It will only include a few kids.
- It will make kids who can't afford them feel bad.

Some **little kids** do not want skateboarding at school because:
- They are afraid of skateboards because they go too fast.
- They think that they won't have any place to play.

The **boys** want skateboarding at school because:
- They like to skateboard. It would keep them busy during recess.
- They won't bug anybody else.
- They will get good exercise.
- They say they will be careful.
- They need something to do.
- They say that skateboarding will help them play sports better.
- They say we allow other sports. Why not have skateboarding?

The **teachers** don't want skateboarding because:
- They don't want to have to settle fights because of kids doing it.
- They think that skateboards cause accidents.
- They think that some kids won't come in from recess on time.
- They say that the classrooms are crowded enough and there is no safe place to store them.
- Only certain kids could skateboard because not all kids can afford them.
- They think that they might get stolen.

Figure 4.6 A third-grade OPV on skateboarding at school

The Repair Suit　　　　　　　　　　　　　　　　　　　　　　　　　　67

Another Perspective-Taking Tool: Analyzing Perspectives

Analyzing Perspectives involves identifying your position or stance on an issue and the reasoning behind that stance. It also involves considering a perspective different from your own. Your perspective on an issue is usually related to some underlying value you hold.[11]

A general strategy to use:

- When you find yourself in a conflict or are upset about something, try to identify your position on the matter at hand.
- Once you have identified your position, try to determine the reasoning behind it.
- Next, try to identify the opposing position.
- Finally, try to describe the reasoning behind the opposing position.

The process may be stated in simpler terms for young students:

- What do I believe about this?
- Why do I believe it?
- What is another way of looking at it?
- Why might someone else believe that?

The Adapted Value Examination Matrix

The *Value Examination Matrix* adapted here is another tool from the Dimensions of Learning. It is simply a structured way for students to analyze perspectives (see Figure 4.7).

1. Statement, Concept or Issue: Maintaining the 55-mph speed limit in Oregon	
2. Assigned Value **For**: I think it is a good idea to maintain the 55-mph speed limit throughout Oregon.	3. Assigned Value **Against**: I think that it is not a good idea to maintain the 55-mph speed limit throughout Oregon. I think the speed limit should be increased.
2a. Reasoning or Logic Behind My Value: • Research shows that maintaining the lower speed limit will save lives. • Roads in the Cascade and the Coast Range Mountains are not designed to accommodate that speed. • People travel faster than the posted speed limit. If the speed limit were increased to 70 mph, we all know that the average speed traveled would be 75 to 78 mph.	3a. Reasoning or Logic Behind My Value: • Many Oregon roads are less traveled and can handle the higher speeds. • The interstate highways can easily accommodate those who desire to travel more quickly and those who desire to travel more slowly. • Newer vehicles are designed to travel safely and efficiently at higher speeds.

1. Identify the rule, concept, or issue to be analyzed. Record it in the top box numbered 1.
2. Take a position either for or against the statement, concept, or issue. Write that position in boxes 2 or 3.
3. Then record your reasoning or logic behind your position in 2a or 3a. After completing your position, take the opposite or an alternative position and analyze it.

Figure 4.7　　The adapted value examination matrix

Identify the rule, concept, or issue to be analyzed. Record it in the top box. Take a position either for or against the statement, concept, or issue. Write that position in boxes 2 or 3. Then record your reasoning or logic behind your position in 2a or 3a. After completing your position, take the opposite or an alternative position and analyze it.

When Naiveté Is the Issue

When naiveté is the issue, give students as many experiences with the subject matter as possible. It is critical to provide multiple examples of the concept at hand and to create an experiential context in which the student maximizes the use of all senses. The following is a tool you can use to facilitate this process.

PMI: Plus, Minus, Interesting

Another tool that can be used to address and challenge or validate current conceptions is *PMI: Plus, Minus, Interesting.* It is another tool from the CoRT Thinking Skills Program.[12]

When using PMI: Plus, Minus, Interesting, students are encouraged to identify the *Pluses:* listing why they think the idea is a good one—why it is sound. They then identify the *Minuses:* listing why they think the idea is not a good one—why it is unsound. Usually, when brainstorming, someone identifies a factor about the idea that, from their point of view, is neither a plus nor a minus. This is what DeBono calls *Interesting*—something to think about but not clearly identified as a plus or a minus.

The purpose of using this tool is to teach students to examine various factors—not just the things they like about the idea. When students use PMI, they learn to look at the idea first before making a judgment, to avoid rejecting an idea that may appear weak at first sight and to look at the disadvantages of an idea that they like very much.

When Inadequate Vocabulary Is the Issue

Obviously, teaching the needed vocabulary is critical to successful understanding. The question becomes: Where should vocabulary be taught? We feel strongly that this must occur at both the First Dare and Repair stages. We suggest that you start in the Prepare stage by using the *Vocabulary Planning Matrix* (see chapter 2). In the First Dare stage-use the tools Click and Clunk and the *Four Square Conceptual Box* (see chapter 3). An effective tool that you can use at the Repair stage is the *LINCS* strategy developed at the University of Kansas.[13]

This strategy is designed particularly for use with learning disabled students but is effective to use with all students. And the beauty of it is that it can be used across the curriculum areas.

There are five steps in the *LINCS* strategy for learning a new vocabulary word:

    L—List the parts

    I—Imagine a picture

    N—Note a reminding word

    C—Construct a LINCing story

    S—Self-Test

Students are given a 3 in. x 5 in. index card on which they draw a horizontal line front and back. On the top of one side, they record the vocabulary word to be learned and circle it. On the top half of the back of the card, they write important parts of the definition.

In step two of the strategy, the student imagines a picture related to the word and shares it with a partner. Next, students are asked to create a "reminding word," a word that may sound similar to the vocabulary word and record it on the bottom half of side one of the card (under the definition).

Students then create a short LINCing story that shows the relationship of the key word and the reminding word. Students take time to include important elements of the definition.

Step five involves students testing themselves on the word meaning by reviewing the card and then sharing the definition. Note that the LINCing strategy can be used as both a First Dare and Repair tool.

Moving From the Minutiae to the Big Picture

Many times, students get so caught up in daily unit activities that they have difficulty moving from the details to the big picture. One tool that Barry Lane devised is very effective in helping students to do this. He calls the tool *ThoughtShots*.[14] We have adapted it here.

ThoughtShots

This tool is designed to help students sophisticate their thinking about the topic. The Thoughtshots tool is used when one needs to rise above the experiential details and identify/articulate the concept or generalization related to the experience. Lane uses the metaphor of "the mountain of perception and the sea of experience" to describe this. We all swim in the sea of experience and at times leave the water, climb the mountain, look down on the sea, and perceive the significance.

To teach this tool, read a passage, view a film clip, or make an oral presentation to the class about a character in which there is an evident character trait being portrayed without the author/presenter being explicit in the text/

presentation. After the presentation, ask students to imagine themselves rising above the scene, taking a look at the "big picture," and identifying the underlying message or theme.

After acquiring new information through viewing, reading, hands-on manipulating, or listening, students' first task may be to identify the important details about the presentation. Following the task of getting the "basics" down, ask students to use their ThoughtShots tool and pull together in one sentence or two the big idea present here.

The Tip of the Iceberg

This Wild Card was developed by Betty to encourage revision and refinement of conceptual understanding. It is primarily a Repair tool, but it can be used throughout the unit to help students track the evolution of their thinking. When students use the tool, they are instructed to monitor and express the changes in their conceptual understanding.

Teachers first start by posting a large blackline of an iceberg in the classroom and discuss with the class the metaphor of how the brain is like an iceberg (see Figure 4.8).

Here are some points that you may want to make in this discussion:

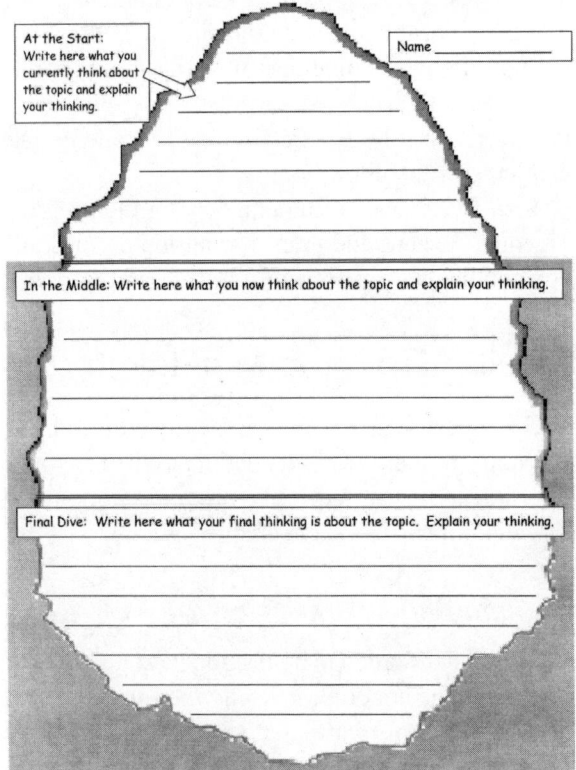

Figure 4.8 The tip of the iceberg

- The bulk of the iceberg is below the surface of the water and invisible from view at first glance.
- A person's brain is like the iceberg in that it contains a great deal more than what the person might share with others.
- As you submerge to examine the iceberg under the surface, you will notice that it is larger than the surface on the top. This is because the

part that is exposed to the wind and the sun melts. Whereas, the part under the water melts much more slowly.

- Sometimes you have learned something and stored it in your brain. This information may be correct or may be wrong. Just like it is easier for the part of the iceberg that is above the surface to change, it is easier to change your thinking about a topic when it is exposed—that is, when you share it, examine it, and discuss it with others.

- In this unit, we are going to start with what you know right now about (*concept/topic*) and then dive deep to expose, share, and examine your understanding so that you can learn more and better information about (*concept/topic*).

Following the discussion, give students a blackline of an iceberg (see Figure 4.9). Have them: (a) record their names at the top, (b) add the name of the concept above the surface of the iceberg, and (c) fold the iceberg at the double lines into three sections so that the top panel (with the name spot) is visible on the top fold.

Instruct students to record their initial thinking about the concept/topic on the top third of the paper—the tip of the iceberg. Remind students that this is just the tip of their thinking and learning. To reinforce that this is just the tip of their thinking, you may have students make an additional fold—that is, fold the top third in half again so that the very top of the iceberg is standing up vertically from the rest of the fan fold. Collect the icebergs and save them.

At some time in the middle of the unit, pass out the icebergs again. Ask students to dive under the surface, to think a minute about their current understanding of the concept, compare it to the originally recorded tip, make any mental revisions to their thinking and record it in the middle section of the blackline. Again collect the figures.

At the end of the unit, pass out the icebergs one more time. Ask students to dive even deeper under the surface, bring up their best, current thinking about the concept, pull it all together and record it on the bottom third of the iceberg. Discuss with the class any changes that occurred in thinking over time.

Here are some possible adaptations. The first time you use the tool with students, we recommend that you complete one on the bulletin board. After students have recorded on their iceberg tips, have a brief discussion with the whole class and record a statement representing a sampling of their ideas on the wall chart.

If you desire, you can have students partner up with one another at each stage, discuss their responses with each other, and then add any additional details resulting from the discussion.

The Conceptual Change Model (CCM)

Posner, Strike, Hewson, & Gertzog (1982)[15] and Strike & Posner (1985)[16] have studied the conditions that must be present in order to bring about conceptual change in students' thinking. These conditions are

- The students must be dissatisfied with their existing views.
- The new conception must appear somewhat plausible.
- The new conception must be more attractive.
- The new conception must have explanatory and predictive power.

Joseph Stephans,[17] professor at the University of Wyoming, developed the *CCM (Conceptual Change Model)* as a method of presenting science concepts to students in such a way that they become aware of their own perceptions, confront them, and change them.

In his book, Stephans shares several single concepts and related concepts around which students consistently hold misconceptions. He then presents the model and describes examples of how it can be used in the science classroom. The CCM consists of six stages.

1. Students *become aware* of their own preconceptions about a concept by thinking about it and making predictions (committing to an outcome) before any activity begins.
2. Students *expose their beliefs* by sharing them, initially in small groups and then with the entire class.
3. Students *confront their beliefs* by testing and discussing them in small groups.
4. Students work toward *resolving conflicts* (if any) between their ideas (based on the revealed preconceptions and class discussion) and their observations, thereby *accommodating the new concept.*
5. Students *extend the concept* by *making connections* between the concept learned in the classroom and other situations, including their daily lives.
6. Students are encouraged to *go beyond,* pursuing questions and problems of their choice related to the concept.

Refer to Stephans' text for several strong examples of this tool in use in the physical sciences; for example, in changing concepts about density, air pressure, and matter.[18]

Oodles of Noodles

Our friend and colleague, Paul Weill, invented this **Repair** tool. It is a tool a teacher can use to help students identify the relationships among the importance of ideas. This is an especially powerful tool to use with younger students who often need concrete representations to anchor their thinking.

Purchase three types of noodles of various sizes for use in this activity. We recommend you use lasagna, fettuccini, and spaghetti. Each will represent the importance of ideas with the widest (lasagna) representing those ideas of key importance, the middle sized (fettuccini) as the next important idea, and the thinnest (spaghetti) as the least important ideas. Place three or four pieces of each type of pasta in a resealable clear baggy. Make enough sets for use by the class, working in small groups of three or four. Of course, if you prefer, you can create pictures of different types of pasta, laminate the pictures, and use them over and over again.

List a number of ideas from the reading, the viewing, the lecture, and so forth, on sentence strips. These can be word processed, enlarged on 11 in. x 17 in. paper and cut into strips.

Have students form into groups of three or four. Give each group a complete set of sentence strips and one baggy full of strips of pasta. Have students work together to determine the ranking of ideas. When the group comes to consensus about one idea, have them cover the strip with the appropriate pasta.

Ask students to start by identifying the most important idea/s and labeling them. Stop and discuss which ideas were selected. Help those groups who may have selected less important ideas to understand the reasoning behind the appropriate selections. Then move onto the next important ideas and the least important ideas.

Students in a second-grade class were given a set of sentence strips from the first chapter of Roald Dahl's book, *Fantastic Mr. Fox*. They worked in small groups to rank the ideas as they relate to each farmer and in order of importance. Figure 4.9 is an example of their work.

When the Locus of Attention Is Elsewhere

There are many reasons why a student's locus of attention is elsewhere. Some of these reasons are beyond our control to address in school. However, quite often you can increase student attention and focus by using simulations. Simulations in the classroom are true learning adventures where students role-play various scenarios.

You may remember hearing the oft-quoted phrase:

> Tell me, I forget.
> Show me, I remember.
> Involve me, I understand.

Name __Shelby__

Cut the noodle boxes out at the bottom of this page. Paste the lasagna noodle by the most important ideas. Paste the fettuccini noodle by the next important ideas. Paste the spaghetti noodle by the least important ideas.

List Ideas Here	Paste noodles here.
Bunce was a pot-bellied dwarf.	Least Important Idea
Bunce ate goose-liver doughnuts.	Least Important Idea
Bogis was a chicken farmer.	Least Important Idea
Boggis and Bunce and Bean / One fat, one short, one lean / These horrible crooks / So different in looks / Were nonetheless equally mean.	Most Important Idea
Bean dosn't eat anything.	Least Important Idea

Figure 4.9 Oodles of noodles worksheet

That is why, as stated earlier in this chapter, simulations provide powerful experiences for students to construct meaning around key content knowledge. Using simulations creates an open-ended and stimulating environment in which students can confront their prior knowledge, identify areas of cognitive dissonance, and pursue deeper and more meaningful understanding. For a number of years, there have been ready-to-go packaged simulations for sale. One of the oldest and most popular is the Interact Company. Another effective simulation model can be found in the Scottish Storyline Design method.[19] There are also a number of great Web sites that provide students with online simulations. We suggest that you do a search using the key words "simulations" and "K–12 education." The following Web sites are excellent resources for simulations.

http://www.roleplaysim.org/papers/

http://www.acs.ilstu.edu/faculty/dldoss/yurcik/nsfteachsim/simteachingresources.html

http://www.insead.edu/CALT/Encyclopedia/Education/Advances/games.html

http://www.interact-simulations.com/

It is important to infuse strategic reflection times into these simulations. These are orchestrated moments where the action stops and reflection and dialogue occur. You could

- Stop the action and ask for a *five-minute write*. You, as the teacher, could provide a specific prompt for the writing, or you could simply have students record their current thoughts about the concept being studied. It is a must to collect the five-minute writes and review them so that you can address any persistent misconceptions in the following teaching.

- Stop and *Huddle.* Have students circle up and discuss the action. Use question cues to elicit current thinking about the concept at hand. Take time to challenge, or further develop, any noteworthy statements.

- Use an *Umbrella Tella*.

Umbrella Tella

Using Umbrella Tella is a graphic way to represent the relationship of larger metaconcepts to their related subconcepts and facts. We label it a Wild Card because it can be used throughout the unit. It is an excellent tool to help students revise their thinking as they move through the unit.

When using the Umbrella Tella with younger students, bring a large umbrella into the classroom to use. If using an actual umbrella may be too "hokey" for older students, they may work exclusively from the blackline master of the umbrella rather then a real one (see Figure 4.10).

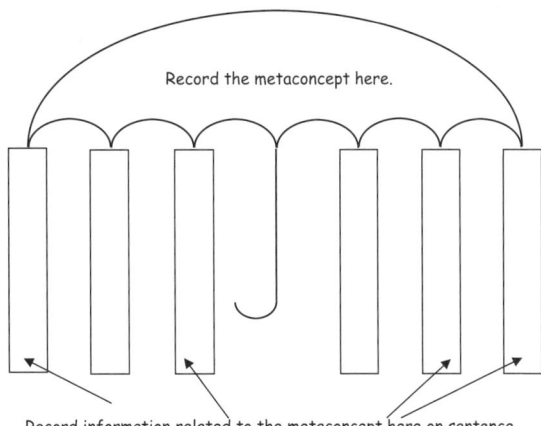

Figure 4.10 The umbrella tella blackline

At the beginning of the unit, attach the metaconcept on the main body of the umbrella with safety pins. On strips of paper, have students write sentence strips that express any related information and suspend them to the main body of the umbrella with safety pins. The goal is to hang several related subconcepts and facts around the umbrella's edge. Make no judgments about the accuracy or quality of the responses.

Throughout the unit, as students acquire new content understanding through reading, listening, viewing, or hands-on manipulating, allow them to remove, revise, and recreate sentence strips for the Umbrella Tella. At the end of the unit, each student can be asked to complete a paper/pencil Umbrella Tella to summarize what they have learned.

During this strategic reflection break, you may get out the actual umbrella and see if any revision needs to be made on the sentence strips.

When Faulty Teaching Is the Issue

When faulty teaching is occurring, one appropriate intervention would be to provide adequate and timely professional development to teachers teaching in these areas. We won't address this issue in depth here. Suffice it to say, the strategies identified above for teaching both procedural and declarative knowledge should be applied in all professional development models. In addition, we encourage the use of a systemic staff development model that involves learning concepts and new methodology, trying them out in the classroom with supervision and coaching, and with continued opportunities for refinement and coaching.

So, Where Are We Now?

In chapter 4, we set out to share a number of Repair tools that you could use in your classroom to help students use fixing-up, evaluating, analyzing, and perspective-taking strategies. We also took you through a *Theory Stop* on the three kinds of knowledge and teaching to the three types of knowledge. Let's summarize the tools we have learned here.

Coming up in chapter 5, we will teach you a number of tools you can use to help students to synthesize and to share their learning. Before you move on to the next chapter, take a minute to reflect on these new tools and identify one or two that you would like to try out in your next unit.

The Repair Suit 77

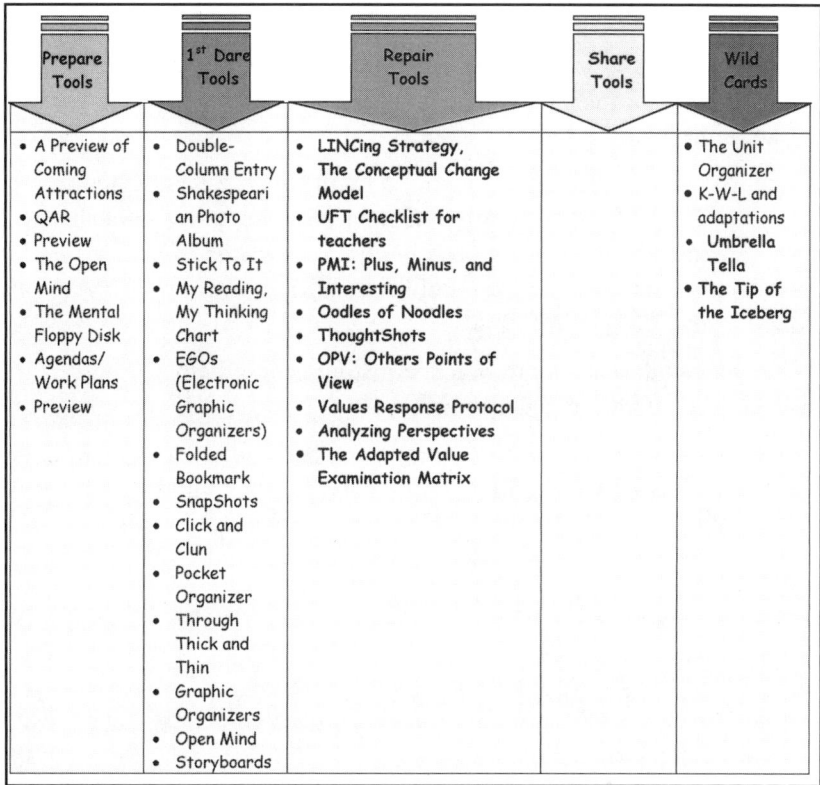

Figure 4.11 Teaching devices introduced in chapter 4

End Notes

1. Marzano, R. J. (1994). *The systematic identification and articulation of content standards and benchmarks.* Aurora, Colorado: Mid-Continent Regional Education Laboratory.

2. A good book to read more about think aloud strategies is *Improving comprehension with think-aloud strategies,* by Jeffrey D. Wilhelm. It was published by Scholastic Publishers in 2001.

3. There is a great site on the Web on schema theory. It is http://www.sil.org/lingualinks/literacy/ImplementALiteracyProgram/SchemaTheoryOfLearning.htm. It is hosted by SIL International (formerly known as the Summer Institute of Linguistics) to work with language communities worldwide to facilitate language-based development through research, translation, and literacy.

4. Marzano, R. J. (1992). *A different kind of classroom: Teaching with the dimensions of learning.* Alexandria, Virginia: Association for Supervision and Curriculum Development, p. 98.

5. See the recommended simulation Web sites in this chapter.

6. An excellent source of information in this area is the book, *Textbooks and the students who can't read them,* by Jean Ciborowski, Brookline Books, Cambridge, Massachusetts, 1992.

7. The FLASH Curriculum was written by the Seattle-King County Department of Public Health, Family Planning Program and is published as *Beyond reproduction: Tips and techniques for teaching sensitive family life education issues,* by Network Publications, a division of ETR Associates, 1983, Santa Cruz, California.

8. We work with teachers to practice distinguishing between universal and nonuniversal/controversial topics.

9. DeBono, E. (1986). *CoRT thinking, Breadth.* New York: Pergamon Press. The reader is encouraged to examine and use the entire CoRT Thinking Skills Program.

10. Ibid.

11. Marzano, ibid.

12. DeBono, ibid.

13. Ellis, E. (1992). *The LINCS strategy training guide.* Lawrence, Kansas: Edge Enterprises.

14. Adapted from: Lane, B. (1993). *After the end: Teaching and learning creative revision.* Portsmouth, New Hampshire: Heinemann.

15. Posner, G., Strike, K., Hewson, P., & Gertzog, W. (1982). Accommodation of a scientific conception: Toward a theory of conceptual change. *Science Education, 66,* 211–227.

16. Strike, K., & Posner, G. (1985). A conceptual change view of learning and understanding. In L. West and A. Pines (Eds.), *Cognitive structure and conceptual change.* Orlando, Florida: Academic Press.

17. Stephans, J. (1994). *Targeting students' science misconceptions, Physical science activities using the conceptual change model.* Riverview, Florida: The Idea Factory.

18. Stephans, ibid.

19. Refer to the book, *Creating worlds: Constructing meaning,* by Jeff Creswell and Bobbi Fisher, for a detailed description of the Scottish Storyline Method. It was published by Heinemann in Portsmouth, New Hampshire, in 1997.

CHAPTER
FIVE

The Share Suit: Show What You Are Learning

"To Cash in One's Chips"

In playing cards with chips, this literally means to take one's chips to the teller and trade them for money. The idiom generally means to sell something for a profit. We want students to collect a number of chips—show what they are learning—as the lesson or unit progresses. We then want them to pull them all together in one or more substantive projects at the end of the unit that is an orchestrated demonstration of their learning.

Larry's Story

"Class, remove all your books, notebooks, and other materials from your desk and place them on the floor. All you need is a pencil to take this unit test."

My students responded predictably. I didn't even have to look. Most groaned, because they knew from prior knowledge that test taking is a drag. A few students smiled inwardly because they were the *A* students who knew the material, knew how to take tests, and knew their precious *A*s would be preserved. Others just sat and stared glumly, because they knew from prior experience about the pain of failing previous tests.

Sadly, all categories of the above students did not really understand that the pencil and paper test was a "test" of their understanding—that is, an investigation into their content acquisition conducted by the teacher as "expert" on that content. In the eyes of our students, tests have become a necessary evil associated with going to school. They do not view tests as "sharing" what they understand; rather, they view them as guessing what the teacher wants and thereby "getting it right."

Theory Stop: From the Saber-Toothed Curriculum to the Share Combo Special

Years ago, Betty came across a little book about teaching, learning, and progressive education that was first published in 1937. It is titled, *The Saber-Toothed Curriculum*.[1] The book, written under the pseudonym of Professor Abner J. Peddiwell by educator Harold Benjamin, satirizes educators and how they cope with change. Professor Peddiwell presents a series of lectures on the content of the curriculum in the paleolithic era. According to Pediwell, the paloelithic curriculum included fish-grabbing-with-the-bare-hands, horse-clubbing, and saber-tooth-tiger-scaring-with-fire. In the satire, even though fish became too agile to catch with the bare hands and horses and tigers disappeared, schools nevertheless went on teaching these traditional subjects.

Why mention *The Saber-Toothed Curriculum* here? Well, from education's humble beginnings, teachers have always struggled with what the appropriate curriculum ought to be and in what ways students should be expected to "share" their understandings. Regardless of the content of the curriculum, sharing understanding is the essential ingredient in the teaching-learning equation. Without knowing what our students know, how can we determine what learning has/partially has/has not occurred?

The saber-toothed curriculum spoof reminds us that assessment used to be exclusively *performance*-based. When a young person demonstrated his learning of how to catch-fish-with-the-bare-hands, the appropriate assessment was: Can you show that you can catch fish with your bare hands? No clearing of the desk. These children were educated through imitation and apprenticeship.

After the early Egyptians and Sumerians invented systems of writing, sharing took a whole new twist. By necessity, students needed to learn to read and write; and when asked to share, they expressed themselves in writing.

Ancient Athenian boys received their education by attending a government-sponsored *gymnasium*. Students held discussions to improve their speaking and their ability to reason. Advanced gymnasiums were formed to teach rhetoric and philosophy. Speaking and reasoning well became those most-valued forms of sharing.

During the Middle Ages, monastery and cathedral schools taught a similar curriculum to the ancient Greeks. Subjects were divided into the "trivium," consisting of grammar, rhetoric, and logic; and the "quadrivium," consisting of such disciplines as mathematics, astronomy, and harmonics. A student who spent his first formal years of education in the trivium was expected to speak audibly and intelligibly, use his wit quickly, and say what he had to say elegantly, eloquently, and persuasively.

Of course, these early teachers had one thing going for them: They did not have masses of students to instruct. Their class size could be as small as one student. So, they had the luxury of *conversing* with each student at length.

So why do schools today have an overreliance on writing with paper and pencil? Educating the masses. When universal public education was embraced by societies, class sizes increased and educators were faced with the need to develop mechanisms to move the masses through the system. In our own United States, these mechanisms used cheap paper and pencils and incorporated selected response "share" techniques, including the bubble test, the unit or chapter multiple-choice test, the essay test, or even the book report, all of which have assisted the teaching-learning process for at least the last hundred years.

We actually are quite excited with the direction that educators are currently taking in the area of classroom-based assessment. Clearly, we are accepting the notion that there is "no one right way" to share what one has learned; that, in fact, there are many right ways to share. You might say that today you can serve up a "share combo special." Students can share what they have learned by sometimes writing, sometimes speaking, sometimes graphically representing, and by sometimes combining all of these modes.

Plus, these "combos" offer more flexibility for students to reveal what they actually think about the content rather than simply "regurgitating" what they think the teacher wants to hear. To spur our students on to honest, motivated, enthusiastic sharing of their learning, we must offer them a new menu of activities to supplement the traditional paper-and-pencil tests. And we will.

We have collected a wide range of "share" tools from teachers across the country that have the advantages of newness, of encouragement, and of deep information processing—just what "sharing" requires.

Writing to Share: "Info Out"

In our earlier chapters, we have offered teaching tools that assist student preparation (chapter 2), student first daring (chapter 3), and student repairing (chapter 4). All of the teaching tools presented are intended to facilitate "Info In," the learning of new content information. Now, our attention shifts to "Info Out"—the revealing of student understanding of that newly learned information.

And, just as with "Info In" presented in the earlier chapters, we will be very aware of employing a multiple-mode approach with "Info Out." That is, the tools designed to promote sharing will play to different student strengths. They come in four different *modes*:

- Written expression
- Vsual representations
- Oral speaking
- Constructed projects

Providing different modes for exposing one's understanding addresses different learning styles. It is obvious that some students excel at writing while others try to avoid it; some kids love to draw and illustrate; some even enjoy speaking to a group; and some like the challenge of big-time construction projects. In this chapter, we will offer variety to provide both opportunity and incentive for all learners to reveal their understanding. Remember, we want them to "collect chips and cash them in for a profit."

Secondly, by using different modes of expression, we can resist the trap of overreliance on writing. Not to say that writing is not a useful "share" mode—it is very useful. We all struggle with balancing a variety of assessments with the reality of class size, and writing helps us here. But because writing is so useful, it is often overused.

Thirdly, whichever "share" mode is used, the students will be applying a set of share strategies recommended back in chapter 2: integrating strategies, organizing strategies, and presenting strategies. By applying these strategies, students will be better able to demonstrate their content understanding—to share what they know.

So, we will not only use writing tools for "Info Out," we will also use visual/graphic/pictorial tools, oral/speaking tools, and construction/project tools. (The latter having been addressed in detail in our earlier book, *Great Performances*, chapter 6, pages 103–139.)

Having reminded ourselves of that, we will begin with . . . writing. And not writing to fill-in-the-blank.

Quick Writes

All teachers know the benefits of using writing for "Info Out." Writing is a critically important skill that all students must practice. Writing is "thinking on paper." And thirdly, writing allows for later evaluation; teachers can read student written work after school, in the evening, or over the weekend. (Sorry, but true.) It has become the primary "share" vehicle in many classrooms.

Let's begin with a category of writing we call "Quick Writes." These are fast writing tools that won't take much class time. Plus, these quickies are motivating, inspiring, and even fun.

THE POSTCARD

This tool is so effective that it should have become overused in schools. But it has not, probably because postcard writing is a dying art in our culture . . . currently being replaced by e-mail? It deserves to be remembered when we want our students to share some information. Kids like writing postcards. Why? They are something not typically assigned in class, so they have the benefit of novelty. Additionally, they are short. Short is good. (Short is also good for teachers who have lots of grading to lug home each evening.) And finally, postcards can be linked to the visual/graphic/illustrative mode by turning the card over and drawing a picture (thus, the picture postcard).

Postcard topics are infinite. Math students can write a postcard to share a math process they learned or a problem they have solved. Or, they can write a reflective postcard about their perceived math strengths and weaknesses.

To whom might math students address their postcards? To each other, explaining how to do "borrow" in subtraction, how to find equivalent fractions, or how to solve for X. Or they can address their postcard to their math teacher. How about writing to their parent/guardian for some school-to-home communication?

Language Arts/English classrooms are perfect settings for post card writing. Students can write to characters in a novel or short story, they can write to authors providing feedback, or they can pretend to be a character in fiction and write to a classmate impersonating another character.

Social Studies teacher Terry Osgerby, Spirit Lake, Iowa, assigns his seventh graders to write a series of five postcards about Mexico. And to encourage success, he leaves little to chance for confusion in the directions (see Figure 5.1).

NAME _____

CLASS _____

Objective: Create 5 postcards; one for each day of a vacation trip to Mexico.

Write a series of postcards from a vacation trip to Mexico. Pick the attractions or sites you would visit after researching Mexico.

On one side of each postcard, write a description of what you have seen or done as if you were writing home to your parents.

On the other side, you will draw, paint, or illustrate with some media of your choice what you have written about.

Materials needed: 3 x 5 cards or self-made 3 x 5 sheets of drawing paper, color markers, color pencils, color pens, color paints, or any other medium (e.g., clip art, computer generated art), research notes of Mexico.

Figure 5.1
Mexico postcards

Postcards not only stimulate communication about content learning, they also require brevity of thought. The size limitation of postcards enforces getting to the point, not dawdling through any filler details. (See Appendix for Postcard Template.)

This reminds us of the "Think Shrink" and "Express Train" techniques developed by Barry Lane, author, speaker, and creator of "Discovery Writing."[2] These tools can be very useful in helping students to write good postcards.

Think Shrink is a tool designed to get students to compress their writing. It is a particularly effective tool to use with students who "go on and on and on." As a class, take an example of writing that is long and contains repetitive phrasing, and have the class work together to identify the boring parts and shrink them into a sentence or two. For example, a page-long description of an event, such as a hike in the country ("We went there. Then we did this. We went there and then we did this. And then we went there and did this. . . ." Anyone else have students who write like this?) This passage might evolve into, "After a long, hard hike, we fell onto the ground from exhaustion."

The Express Train notion involves having students get out a bunch of ideas and then "take the express train" through them to write a draft with the essence of the experience. This type of writing is particularly helpful when one is expected to identify the key points from pages of more detailed writing; that is, get the "big picture" from the minutiae.

The good news about postcards is that they teach students how to "shrink" what they will share—that is, to prioritize information; the bad news is that this ranking and selection of information is difficult for some to do. Therefore, we suggest modeling to students how to write a succinct, effective postcard to an audience with a purpose of communicating information. Perhaps the teacher could conduct a "think aloud," whereby he or she talks out loud about the choices being made to the class while demonstrating how to write a postcard. The teacher reveals his or her thinking to the students. It is smart teaching to make no assumptions that the post card is a simple, easy assignment for all students.

An alternative writing assignment is the memorandum. Students write a memo TO: someone RE: something learned in class. This format is engaging to students because of its novelty. Likewise, it is a motivator because it is short and nonintimidating. Of course, very few students have ever seen, much less written, a memo, so teacher modeling is essential. Memos can be written in the intermediate, middle, and high school grades in place of postcards in the very same ways described above. I, Betty, used them with my primary students when they returned to the classroom from recess. Each day, I might be faced with two or three complaints about what had occurred outside. I simply reminded students that I was interested in helping problem solve around the issue/s but that I couldn't do it right then. I charged them with writing a memo to me to explain the situation for later problem solving. They have proven to be popular with students. For a more detailed examination of memo writing, see *Paving the Way in Reading and Writing* (Lewin, 2003).

For primary students, we can integrate literature and writing with *The Jolly Postman: Or Other People's Letters,* by Janet and Allen Ahlberg (Little Brown & Co., September 2001). In this book, an English postman delivers mail to his fairy tale patrons—letters, catalogs, birthday cards, and, yes, a postcard from Jack of beanstalk fame to the Giant. The mail is presented in its true format, so that students can remove the mail from the book. Of course, after the reading of/listening to this engaging literature, young writers compose their own mail to fairy tale characters or, more likely, collaborate to compose a class-written postcard.

THE FIVE-MINUTE WRITE

This is a quickie, even faster than a postcard. For five minutes, students free-write about the assigned topic. That is, they think about what they know about the topic under study, and they record those thoughts on paper.

Obviously, the five-minute write is a First Dare, and it typically remains a First Dare because there is no need to return to it and repair it. It serves as a rough download of content information that has been accumulating in the brain and now is released to paper. That is the purpose of the five-minute write—reveal your thinking. This is great practice for integrating and organizing newly learned content information—two key sharing strategies. The third strategy, presenting, is minimally addressed with this tool. The audience is really yourself. The five-minute write is a chance to reflect on what you are in the process of learning.

Two modifications are possible. First, the teacher can become a second audience of the five-minute write, and read what each student has written. No formal assessment, as in assigning a point score or letter grade, is necessary, as this is a brief "check-in" of understanding.

Secondly, a five-minute write could be revisited later on, so that students would be able to "repair" any statements that may need fixing, supplementing, or removing.

We do not know who invented this technique. We think we learned this from Howard Gardner at a conference. If you know the developer of it, let us know. We would like to give credit for this quick and effective share tool.

THE LETTER

A third relatively quick share tool is the letter. Letter writing in school has been a traditional assignment, but it does not only mean writing to local officials about an issue, to a state tourism board for demographic data, or to a company asking for samples. Letter writing can be used to divulge student understanding of content information—that is, to "info out" what has been "info inned."

For example, students in Lee Burton's class, at Farms School in Hartford, Michigan, exchange letters about their study of Guatemala. As they learn about the history, cultures, and economics during a unit on this country, they compose letters to classmates simulating a "field trip." Mari and Katie reveal their understanding in a back-and-forth give and take (see Figure 5.2).

Dear Katie,

Today I had dinner at a friend's house. Her name is Maria. It was very enjoyable but their houses are so poor. We gave some money to her but she would not accept it. Finally...after begging her to take it because we felt so bad...she took the money. She is a very good weaver. She made some rugs and blankets for me. I asked to see some books of Guatemala. My mistake. She does not have any books. She can't afford them...

Your friend,
Mari

Dear Mari,

Today a lady invited me into her house for dinner... There was only enough food for 2 and there were already 6 not counting me. I felt so helpless. I felt as if someone had cut a hole in me. So empty. I told her that I insist that her family eats the food...I really wanted to stay but it was getting dark...Before I left I was giving her 20 Guatemalan dollars. She wouldn't take it so I left it on her table and quickly left...I had missed the bus so I had to walk...All of a sudden I heard gun shots and several screams. I quickly ran on, there was nothing I could do. The next day I found out that the army killed 9 women because they ate vegetables while working. "This is going to end soon" a lady said but she's been saying it for years.

Love,
Katie

Figure 5.2 Letter exchange

And notice that this share activity occurs *during* the unit of study, not at the end. This is a good reminder that students do not have to wait until the end to expose their knowledge in-progress. In-progress understanding is as valuable as end-of-progress understanding. Using assessment terminology, *formative* assessment is as important as *summative* assessment.

Another letter writing tool is to change the audience from a classmate to a parent. Judy McFadden's students in Mountain Home, Idaho, write a letter home once a month to inform the family about "what I am learning in class." Judy knows that this accomplishes two important things: (a) Now when parents ask, "What did you do in school today?" they have enough concrete information to disbelieve their child's answer, "Nothing," and (b) By composing a letter, students must think about what it is they are learning—a nice review technique. They integrate and organize the information before they present it to their parents/guardians.

Lastly, the teacher can spice up the audience for student letters. Kids can write to literary authors, book characters, scientists, mathematicians, principals, or to another teacher. Ronelda Capadona's sixth graders, at Goodman Elementary School in Chandler, Arizona, wrote to me (Larry) commenting on a teaching idea Ronelda picked up in a workshop I presented. Her students gave me feedback on "Literature Log Codes," a technique that trains student readers how to respond in different ways to a literature selection. Then they invented their own new code (see Figure 5.3).

In all of the above letter writing examples, students are integrating information, organizing it, and presenting it to an audience.

Another use of the letter is to offer it as an opportunity for students to seek help with solving a problem at school. When Betty taught Kindergarten and first grade, she employed a large stuffed animal, Cleo the Cat, to receive letters from her primary students seeking advice. Cleo would read the letters after school and write a personal response to the child, offering a suggested solution.

If Cleo had difficulty reading the handwriting, Betty would approach the child the next day, and in a low voice say, "Cleo had trouble reading this. Will you tell me what you wrote, and I will tell Cleo." This letter-writing tool is effective in creating an inviting, safe, and supportive classroom environment; plus, it provides practice in sharing one's thoughts in writing.

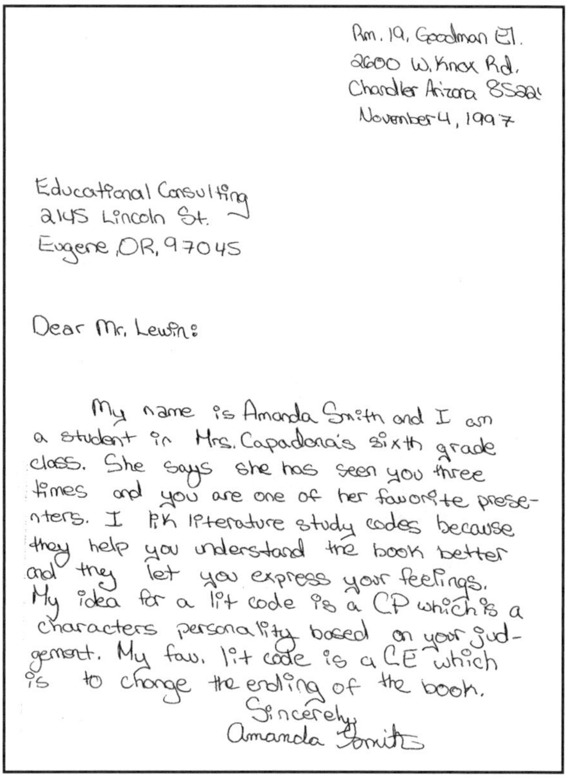

Rm. 19, Goodman El.
2600 W. Knox Rd.
Chandler Arizona 85224
November 4, 1997

Educational Consulting
2145 Lincoln St.
Eugene, OR, 97045

Dear Mr. Lewin:

My name is Amanda Smith and I am a student in Mrs. Capadona's sixth grade class. She says she has seen you three times and you are one of her favorite presenters. I lik literature study codes because they help you understand the book better and they let you express your feelings. My idea for a lit code is a CP which is a characters personality based on your judgement. My fav. lit code is a CE which is to change the ending of the book.

Sincerely,
Amanda Smith

Figure 5.3 Letter about "Literature Log Codes"

With any letter writing assignment, let's not assume that all our students know how to write a letter. Let's structure it, so that everyone understands who the audience is, what the purpose for writing is, and how to organize the information into a letter format.

THE ANNOTATED OPEN MIND

A final "quick" writing tool is the Annotated Open Mind. You met the Open Mind back in chapter 2 as a First Dare tool (page 11). It can also be used as a Share tool if students are required to write more extensively inside the mind template—to make more detailed annotations.

For example, during a history unit on 1492, students learned about the hopes and fears of the Spanish sailors crossing the Atlantic onboard the *Niña, Pinta,* and *Santa Maria.* Kendra shares what she knows with her Open Mind, and her classmate Loretta has so much to share that she filled up the entire template with the thoughts of a sailor (see Figure 5.4).

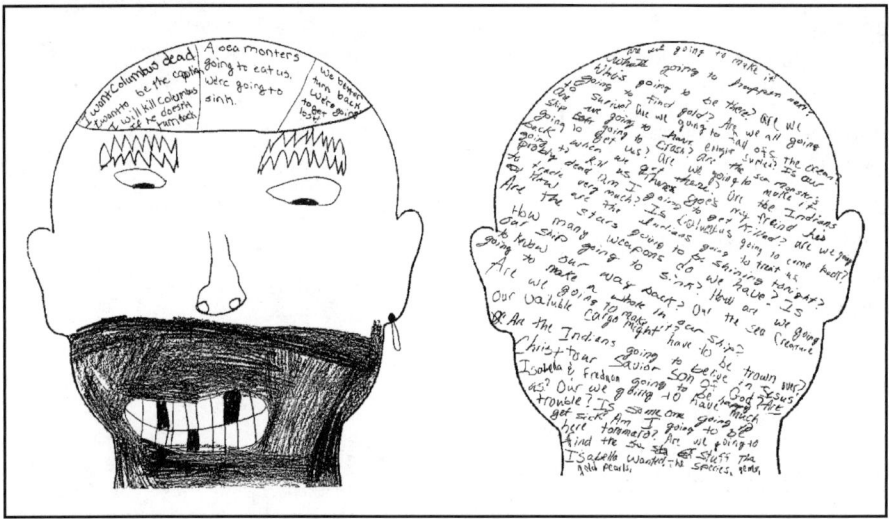

Figure 5.4 An open mind

Open Minds are exceptionally useful in teaching students to view content information from different perspectives. If teaching *points of view* is part of your curriculum, the Annotated Open Mind is worth trying out.

More Formal Writing

Although postcards, letters, and annotated Open Minds are relatively quick for teachers to assign and for students to finish, other writing-mode tools offered are more formal. This next set induces students to take more time in order to produce a more substantial written response. We will consider the brochure, the news article, and the review/critique. This set works well to teach students the third share strategy: presenting.

The Brochure

Brochures are popular in social studies classrooms when the topic is the U.S. states, the Canadian provinces, or another country. Students research the state, province, or country ("Info In") and then report back the culture(s), economics, demographics, and climate in the form of a travel brochure ("Info Out"). This is universally well received by students at various grade levels, due to its novelty, its format, and the role of pictures to accompany words.

But brochure writing is not limited to social studies. Language Arts/Literature teachers Cori Honn and Victoria Lamkey, at Haysville Alternative High School in Haysville, Kansas, have created a brochure template to help their ninth graders as a review tool before beginning to read an assigned novel, such as *To Kill a Mockingbird*. They call it the "Elements of Fiction" brochure. It functions as a lead-in to what to look for and expect (see Figure 5.5).

Figure 5.5 "Element of Fiction" brochure template (outside)

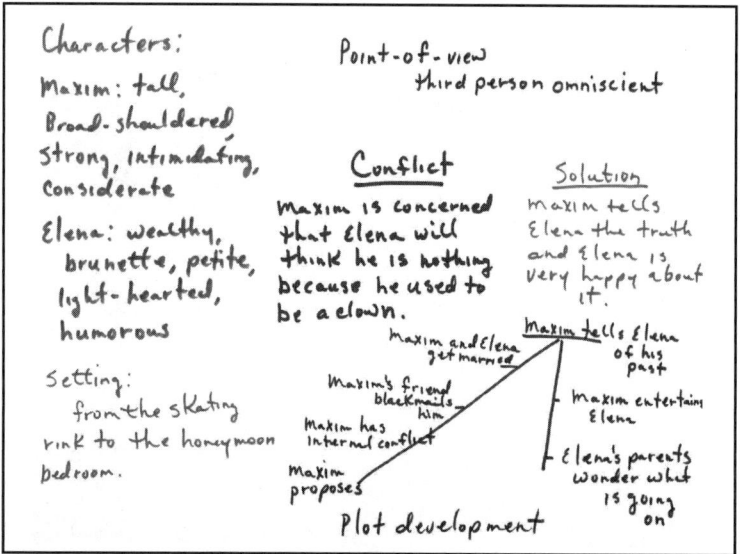

Figure 5.5 "Element of Fiction" brochure template (inside) (*continued*)

Now, teaching students that all fictional pieces have the same elements could be accomplished in different ways. One would be an outline of them in order. Another could be a graphic organizer (concept web) with the elements clustered. But, really, which of the three options would be the most enticing to students? The brochure, for sure. It is important to present kids with something more engaging than what they are used to. And to heighten the enthusiasm, a teacher could collect sample brochures to show as models.

Sue Walters and the seventh-grade team of teachers at Schuylkill Middle School in Leesport, Pennsylvania, designed a seventh-grade integrated unit brochure project on tropical rain forests. As the Language Arts teacher, Sue guided her students through writing a letter to the editor and placed it on the front panel of the brochure. Her colleagues joined in the effort, making it a truly interdisciplinary project.

The foreign language teacher guided the students to label their rain forest drawings in German. The social studies teacher was responsible for rain forest information—both a map and information about the indigenous people living there. The math teacher instructed the students on how to make scale drawings of a rain forest species. And the science teacher "info inned" the students on remarkable rain forest facts.

As if this writing assignment wasn't rich enough, Sue incorporated computer technology by deputizing the computers' word processing program for desktop publishing of the brochures, including using clip art to decorate the brochures (see Figure 5.6). This is a good reminder that while brochures mainly rely on writing to communicate the information, graphics also play a key role. Brochures clearly need visuals to support the words.

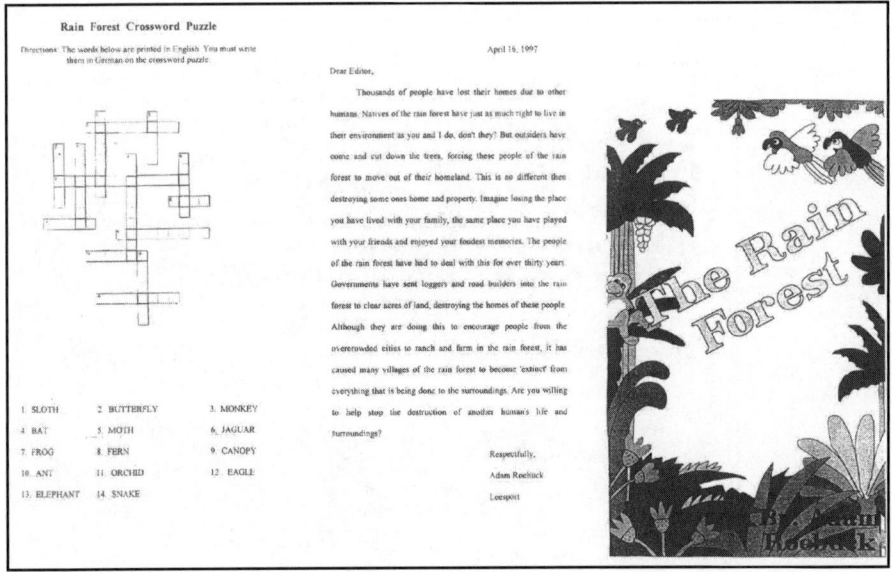

Figure 5.6

The above topics are surely not the only possibilities, but rather serve to stimulate your imagination for brochure writing in your classroom.

Elementary, middle, and high school students like brochures as a means for sharing what they've learned. However, to write a successful brochure by following the teacher's step-by-step directions takes time. We believe it is worth the time, but we certainly are not recommending brochures for every topic or unit that you teach.

If the integration of computer technology interests you, there are a number of software applications that can speed up the use of the brochure tool. Many word processing programs have ready-made brochure templates. Two Microsoft products (Microsoft Word and Publisher) have brochure templates as well as ClickBook software by Blue Squirrel.

The Class Newspaper

This more formal writing tool is best used with students in Grades 5 and above. Although third or fourth graders may be able to write news articles, our examples will be from secondary grade levels.

When I (Larry) taught middle school, I assigned news articles as an "Info Out" tool for U.S. History. For example, after studying the Boston Massacre, students went into the school's computer lab and composed an article for either the *Boston News* or the *London Express.* The neatness of the laser printed articles was impressive to the students, but, of course, not the primary target of the assignment. Rather, it was the content information gleaned from the unit, plus taking a perspective on the event (Colonial or British).

I am certain that the students learned more about this important event by writing an article about it than from memorizing the people, places, and things for a test. And this is a key characteristic of the "Share" stage: The learning continues as the students "Info Out."

Again, we are not opposed to tests. In fact, I gave my class a test on the Boston Massacre to solidify their basic understanding of the event. Then, they took the basic facts and applied them in a new context—the article.

This is an example of a classroom-based performance assessment task; students apply skills and knowledge in a meaningful assignment. For more information on the news article as a performance task, see our earlier book, *Great Performances: Creating Classroom-Based Performance Tasks* (Lewin & Shoemaker, ASCD, 1998).

Susan Strano at Northside Elementary School in Palmyra, Pennsylvania, employed the news article tool with her sixth-grade Social Studies students when they studied Colonial American history. Each student composed an article to be published in a class newspaper. To assess each student, Susan created a 6-point scoring rubric. She evaluated student proficiency at each stage of the writing process: Prepare, First Dare, Repair, and Share. We will check out her rubric later in this chapter, when we address "Sharing as Assessment."

Another use of the news article is Monroe Middle School's eighth-grade culminating project: an autobiographical newspaper created on large sheets of butcher paper. Each graduating eighth grader must author five newspaper articles, including a historical article in Dorothy Syfert's Language Arts/Social Studies Block class.

The assignment is to write an article about a person or event in history that particularly interested and/or affected you. Emmy had been fascinated with the unit on the Salem Witch Trials, so she opted to write about that infamous event. However, to have enough information to include in the article, Emmy needed to review that unit and to conduct additional research.

That is where I (Larry) came in. Having taught next door to Dorothy for nine years, we developed a great partnership. So I occasionally return to coteach with her. I offered to help her class find additional information about their self-selected topics on the Internet's World Wide Web.

I showed the class a set of outstanding educational directories—lists of quality Web sites created by teachers, librarians, and other informed adults. Directories remove the issue of landing at off-topic sites, inappropriate sites, or worse. For more information on the directories versus search engines, see *Using the Internet to Strengthen Curriculum,* Lewin, ASCD, 2000, pages 45–49.

Emmy and her classmates had two class periods to visit directory sites to link to quality sites on their topics. All of this is "Info In."

Check out Emmy's "Info Out" article on "Sarah Good," composed using a computer word processor and formatted into two columns to replicate an actual newspaper article. (Use either a Microsoft Publisher template or an AppleWorks stationery.) It was published in her Autobiographical Newspaper and displayed on the wall of the school's courtyard for graduation ceremonies (see Figure 5.7).

Our local newspaper, the Eugene, Oregon, *Register-Guard,* has a weekly section called "20 Below." Created by a team of local high school, community college, and university students

Sarah Good

On June 10th a inoccent women was hung in Salem Village. The crime that she was accused of was Witchcraft. Nineteen others were convicted of witchcraft and hung in the year to come. Sarah Good was the second women to be tried, convicted and hung of witchcraft in Salem. She was the daughter of an innkeeper. He took his own life when Sarah was only 17 years of age. Her father did leave he an estate of 500 pounds after debt. The estate was to be divided between his widow and her two oldest sons. A portion of the money was to be given to each of their seven daughters when they became of age. Sarah's mother remarried very quickly and as a result her new husband had possession of the estate leaving most of the girls without anything.

When Sarah became older she married an indentured servant by the name of Daniel Poole. He died in the year 1683, leaving only debt to be paid off. Sarah and her second husband were expected to pay it off. By the time of the witch trials, Sarah and her husband were homeless and poor. They had to resort to begging for food and money and when people would not look down at them she would mumble words under her breath, people would think that she was casting a spell on them. At the time of the trials, Sarah's only child was arrested of witchcraft also and confessed to her mother being a witch and that in her mothers influence, she had no choice but to be a witch.

Sarah Good (cond.)

During the trials some of the evidence was false, but at that time they didn't know any better. During one of her examinations, one of the girls stated that she was rite then being stabbed by Good. A broken knife was found on the girl. As soon as the court had examined the knife, a young boy came out and said that he had broken the knife yesterday and he had put the broken piece on the presence on the girls.

Sarah Good was executed on July 19th 1692. She didn't confess to being a witch and showed no worries at her execution. In fact the statement that she stated before her hanging actually became true. She said to Minister Nicholas Noyes,"You are a liar. I am no more a witch than you are a wizard, and if you take away my life the God will give you blood to drink." The wierd thing is that her statement actually came true. Noyes died of internal hemorrhage, bleeding ecesivly at he mouth. So the question I leave you with is, was she really a witch?

Emmy Greatwood

Figure 5.7

under 21 years of age, this Monday section is loaded with interesting articles written by student journalists on topics of interest to young people. Some weeks, the students also write reviews on films, television, and books. If you'd like to read some, visit the Web site at http://www.20Below.com. This offers a broadened audience beyond the teacher. Perhaps your local paper may be interested in starting a student-authored column or section.

Picture Book Critiques

As mentioned earlier, a classic share tool has been the book report. But due to overuse, it often lacks the necessary appeal to engage many students. Plus, it typically served as a retelling, a "spitting back of the book." So, let's consider replacing it with the Book Review.

What's the difference? In a book report, the student only reports back the elements of fiction. The book review goes beyond the retelling to constructing a review—an informed opinion supported with solid reasons. This tool forces the students to climb up a notch on the thinking scale by incorporating all three share strategies: integrating, organizing, and presenting. Plus, in order to form an opinion about the book, students will be coaxed back to *reread* parts of the book to gain specific information to support the opinion. This nicely links the "share" stage with the "repair" stage.

Any assigned fiction can be used to launch the writing of a book review: a novel, a short story, or poem. Tom Dickey's fifth graders, in Albion, Nebraska, wrote critical reviews on children's picture books.

As Tom said, "I think this would be a great idea for teaching critiquing skills for any age level. Everyone loves a good children's book—this will encourage kids to get in there and find out *why* they liked it."

We think Tom is right. Picture books are not written only for primary grade students. Upper elementary, middle, and even high school students are delighted by the hundreds of thousands of outstanding picture books available. But just because students like them, it doesn't automatically mean that they know how to critique them. So Tom made no assumptions. Instead, he provided his class with a "Book Evaluation Form," with nine prompted questions (see Figure 5.8).

BOOK EVALUATION FORM

Your name________________

Title______________________
Author__________________

	YES	NO
Characters (did you care for them?)	___	___
Setting (was it important?)	___	___
(did you feel as if you were there?)	___	___
Was it a story or informational? (circle one)		
Conflict (could you find one? What was it?)	___	___
Message (did it have meaning to you?)	___	___
Illustrations (were they attractive & helpful?)	___	___

Rating (1=poor, 5=fantastic)

1 2 3 4 5

Age/grade level

Write a short summary (You will use this later, so include all names and items you want to include in you're final summary.)

Figure 5.8 Book evaluation form

> **The Eleventh Hour**
> Graeme Base
>
> I picked up a copy of The Eleventh Hour. I'd say the pictures were probably the reason I got it. It's an exquisite story with a huge mystery. The problem is the food is missing and you've got to find who did it! I give this book five stars and I recommend it to ages ten and up. I think Graeme Base did a terrific job on this book.
>
> Mitchell Wolf

Figure 5.9

Employing the benefits of the computers' word processors, his fifth graders completed Evaluations for each of the 10 picture books they selected to read. Then they self-selected three books to write reviews, which were published in the class's "Picture Book Critiques." Mitchell's review is in Figure 5.9.

Besides the three book reviews, each student also created an advertisement poster for a book (visual/graphic mode) and appeared in a videotaped oral book review (speaking mode). The whole package nicely ties writing, speaking, and illustrating together. It is a fine example of a large-scale project—the fourth "Info Out" mode.

Technical Writing

Raising the bar a tad, we will explore another set of writing tools that inspire students to "share." This set requires more intensive writing, because it moves them into the technical writing mode.

A Training Manual

When I (Larry) taught middle school language arts and social studies, I always looked for ways to incorporate writing with content information. And I looked for assignments that would grab my students' attention and gain their energy.

It occurred to me that writing for the purpose of explaining and informing is a motivator for students if they actually know enough about a topic to explain it well. And if the audience for this information is intriguing to them, then we have a powerful "Info Out" tool.

I tried it with my eighth graders. At the beginning of a unit on the 1492 historical period, I told them that they would learn many things that they didn't yet know about Columbus, the Spaniards, and the Taino Indians of the Caribbean. All this new information would be shared with my *next year's* class, so that they could benefit from this class's wisdom. The vehicle for this wisdom sharing was to be a "Technical Training Manual." Joanne Wesener at Howard's Groves Middle School in Cleveland, Wisconsin, learned about this writing task in a workshop I presented, and she immediately figured out how to modify it to fit her teaching situation. Her sixth graders were assigned to compose a Technical Training Manual on "Helpful Hints for Next Year's Language Arts

Students," which was a review of the major class activities for the year. It was a very effective use of writing for sharing (see Figure 5.10).

FROM US TO YOU

THE CLASS OF 2003

21 TIPS ON MAKING MUSEUM BROCHURES!

Museum

* Remember details
* Have fun!
* Make it colorful
* Use creative ideas
* Draw pictures
* Write about what you saw
* Write about the gift shops

Discovery World/I-Max

* Write about activities
* Have fun!
* Draw pictures
* Write about experiments you could do
* Write what you do
* Write how many stories high it was

* Write what movie you saw
* Write about the movie
* Describe how exciting it was
* Write the part you liked best
* Draw colorful pictures
* Be creative
* Have fun!

Fold paper like this:

Kara Reseburg 6-F #16
Laura Ver Straate 6-F #19
Lana Athorp 6-F #1
Anna Calhoun 6-F #4

Figure 5.10

Sharing expertise with other students provides a motivating audience and purpose for writing. And the mode, technical writing, deserves a chance in our curriculum. Most of us agree that technical writing (and reading) will only increase in importance in our society as we move steadily into the new millennium.

Fact to Fiction

Writing in a Language Arts/English class is a natural and frequent act, especially when the reading of literature is involved.

The Short Story

Patrick Crowe, English teacher at LeRoy Central High School in LeRoy, New York, teachers a unit on the short story. Besides reading selected short stories by famous authors, his students must take what they have learned and write *their own* short pieces of fiction.

Writing quality short stories is a most challenging undertaking. To tell an engaging story with absorbing characters who do interesting things in only a few pages is a literary achievement of the highest order.

So naturally, Patrick prepares his students for this assignment by leading them through the elements of fiction, the elements of style, and an analysis of the professional writers they read. Plus, he connects literature to recent American history by requiring that the fictional pieces be *historical* fiction.

The results are impressive. So impressive that he has published the student-authored short stories into classroom volumes entitled, "Senior Stories." Here is an excerpt from Brian's story about the Kent State, Ohio, deaths of student protestors entitled, "A Senseless Killing." Notice that the fiction is supported by history—his references to documented resources (see Figure 5.11).

> The next day, May 4, started out fairly calm. Everyone was still "walking on eggshells" around campus though. William and I had our Human Anatomy 102 course at 10:30 A.M. Through the windows we could see the masses congregating at the Commons. The Commons is a grassy hill in the center of campus. Many of the rallies took place here. There was a throng of people milling around. The National Guard was looming large in the background. Things at this point could get very ugly, but I thought of the limited problems we had yesterday and my mind went back to the lecture.
>
> Class got over with at about quarter of noon and William and I were curious as to what was going on. So we went over to the crowd to see what was up. There was shouting going on between the National Guard and the students. The Guard was politely asking the students to disperse but the students would have none of this. The National Guard started to march at the students. We retreated back to a parking lot behind Taylor Hall {Newsweek, p. 32}. I remember thinking how ridiculous this all was. That should have been my cue to leave but I stayed because William was curious. Students started to throw small rocks at the Guard, this was turning ugly quick. I heard someone yell, "Get the bag of rocks" {U.S. News & World Report, p. 34}. My heart was racing as things took a turn for the worse. Rocks were flying all over the place, the Guard was getting hit. I think some people forgot they possessed loaded weapons. This was getting ridiculous.

Figure 5.11 "A Senseless Killing"

Other classmates chose to write historical fiction accounts of the explosion of the Space Challenger, the Vietnam War, the Oklahoma City Bombing, and the Woodstock music concerts. "Info In" occurred individually for these twelfth graders who self-selected these U.S. history topics. Alternatively, students can "Info In" on a common topic—whatever the teacher is teaching.

Elementary students can also write historical fiction stories. For example, students in Lee Burton's special education class at Farms School in Hartford, Michigan, wrote accounts of Pearl Harbor, the war in Vietnam, and the fourth Ice Age (see Figure 5.12).

> The Ice Age began when snow clouds filled with water from the sea. The snow fell and didn't melt during the summer months. The snow packed together and became glaciers made of ice and snow. Everyday they got larger and started to move. The seas got shallower. During each ice age the water level went down until there was land from Russia to Alaska.
> After the fourth Ice Age about 40,000 years ago, hunters came from Asia to North America chasing animals. The hunters wore warm fur clothes and made spears and tools out of stones, wood and animal bones. They hunted for the wooly mammoth which lived all over North America. The wooly mammoth weighed more than an elephant and it got 17 feet high. The hunters hunted for bison and saber-toothed tigers, too.
>
>
>
> I came from Russia with a group of hunters. We were in Alaska heading south. It was night and we had a bonfire and then we went to sleep. In the middle of the night I heard a noise. It was a loud noise. It was coming from the thick green trees. I got up and my heart was beating faster and faster. My face was turning red. I went to get my spear. Then I walked to the woods and I saw a wooly mammoth. I sneaked up on him. The mammoth didn't see me. I threw my spear at his neck. It dropped to the ground and made that loud noise again. The other hunters heard it that time. They ran up to me and said, "Great job." I pulled my spear out and there was blood all over it. By the time I cleaned my spear it was morning. All the hunters said I was the best hunter there. We used the bones for spears and we used the fur for clothes. It was so cold that we put the meat in the snow. We needed to kill the animal just to survive.
>
> Eleven thousand years ago the ice began to melt. Water was everywhere. Some people found spear points or bones buried where the ice used to be. Bones and spear points tell scientists more about the men of the Ice Age.
>
> Randy
> Grade 5

Figure 5.12 The fourth ice age

Naturally, preparation is essential. Lee provided each student with assistance in acquiring a book or two about a historical event to "Info In" the content. Distributing 3 in. x 5 in. note cards encouraged notetaking skills. He reviewed the proper punctuation of dialogue, knowing that characters in the stories would undoubtedly speak.

To help guide his young authors through the writing process and to monitor their progress toward completion, Lee created a "Monitoring Checklist," with five columns (see Figure 5.13).

SAMPLE MONITORING CHECKLIST FOR HISTORICAL FICTION OR VARIATIONS OF THIS ACTIVITY

ASSIGNMENT: HISTORICAL FICTION

Name	Topic	Note cards	Rough Draft w/highlighting	Final Copy

VARIATIONS

GEOGRAPHY: Geography works extremely well within this process of combining fact and fiction. Instead of researching an historical event or era, the student delves into a geographical region. Students of mine have written stories about places all over the globe. Settings could be within political boundaries (countries, cities, etc.) or in physical regions (deserts, islands, etc.) The process is identical to historical fiction.

CULTURE: Rather than focus on a particular place or time period, the student could examine the culture of another people. Areas of research could include many aspects of culture such as life style, shelter, food, clothing, religion, traditions, family structure, etc. This presents a marvelous opportunity to create a multi-ethnic curriculum.

BIOGRAPHIES: The use of historical figures was recommended earlier in this booklet but repeated here so that it is not overlooked.

Figure 5.13

More Elaborate Writing: The Big Kahunas

Ready for the big time? Elaborate writing assignments require more time and energy. For some teachers, this investment pays off handsomely because of the learning it fosters. We will consider two elaborate writing tools: the Annotated Collection and the *I*-Search.

Annotated Poetry Collection

During a unit of study, students selected materials that were meaningful to them. These materials can be teacher-provided or student-acquired. The point was to collect these resources into a packet and then write about the value of them in the form of comments, reactions, notes, and/or reflections—annotations.

This idea comes from Beth Kolbush at Arcadia High School in Oak Hall, Virginia, who learned it at an NCTE conference, adapted it, and shared with us her twelfth-grade students' Poetry Collections. She instructed her students:

> To deepen your experience with poetry, you will be compiling a collection of poems that are special to you in some way. I am not concerned with where you find your poems, but you must identify the author and the source. The primary concern is that you have chosen examples of good poetry that relate to a theme.
>
> You will write an introduction for your collection. This opening statement will explain not only the theme but also your reasons for choosing to include each of these poems. The introduction should define the focus of what will follow in the collection. Don't be afraid to reflect about the larger issues your poems address or about the nature of poetry itself.

Because Beth knew that none of her students had experience creating such a collection, she provided them with more detailed instructions:

> As you compile your collection, pick five of the poems to write about. Include a paragraph with your reaction to the poem and another for your interpretation of it. You may also comment on rhyme, rhythm, figurative language, metaphor, simile, etc., and the effectiveness in the poems.
>
> When you have gathered all your poems together, decide how you will present them. You may include a cover, artwork, photographs, or computer graphics. Unless you have a reason to arrange them otherwise, place them in this order:
>
> - title page
> - preface
> - five poems
> - your comments
> - another five poems
>
> Make your Poetry collection the best it can be, because I will be sharing it with other classes.

One of her students, Sheena, selected the theme of friendship for her collection. In her Preface, she admitted:

> When this assignment was first given, I thought, "Why me?" Poetry is not one my strong points. Then as I began to search the Web, I found some interesting poems. I also found out that poetry is one thing that can defy most laws of grammar. It gets away with these errors because most people's poems are much deeper [on meaning] than how they arranged it, capitalization, punctuation, etc.

While the Annotated Collection is perfect for poetry, it is not limited to only this genre. Students could collect short stories, essays, and articles on a theme or topic, compile them, and write about them as annotations.

The I-Search

At the beginning of this chapter, we criticized the traditional research report for being overused and underinspiring. But we didn't dismiss it entirely, because we know that it still has a place in the curriculum for many students—on many subjects—at different grade levels.

We recommend packaging the report into a format we learned as the "I-Search." (We would like to cite the original author of this notion, but don't know where it came from.) This structures the daunting task of researching a topic into a problem-solving process approach. You won't be surprised that the process includes four steps: Prepare, First Dare, Repair, and Share. We have advocated the use of these four steps throughout this book, and we strongly recommend applying them to the most elaborate writing assignment: the research report. See Figure 5.14 for a detailed look at each stage.

Betty has used the I-Search method with first graders. Of course, students conducted the research as a "we" search—that is, in a group. Here is how it went.

> First, I had a context in which to interest students in doing basic research. Each year in my classroom, I would display a number of agates and other stones I had gathered from the Oregon coast. Students were also encouraged to add to the collection. We then set up a rock tumbler in class to polish the rocks.
>
> Students always had a number of questions about the collection. They included
>
> - Why are some rocks smoother than others?
> - Why are some see-through and others not see-through?
> - What happens in the tumbler?
> - Why do some rocks get very small in the tumbler?

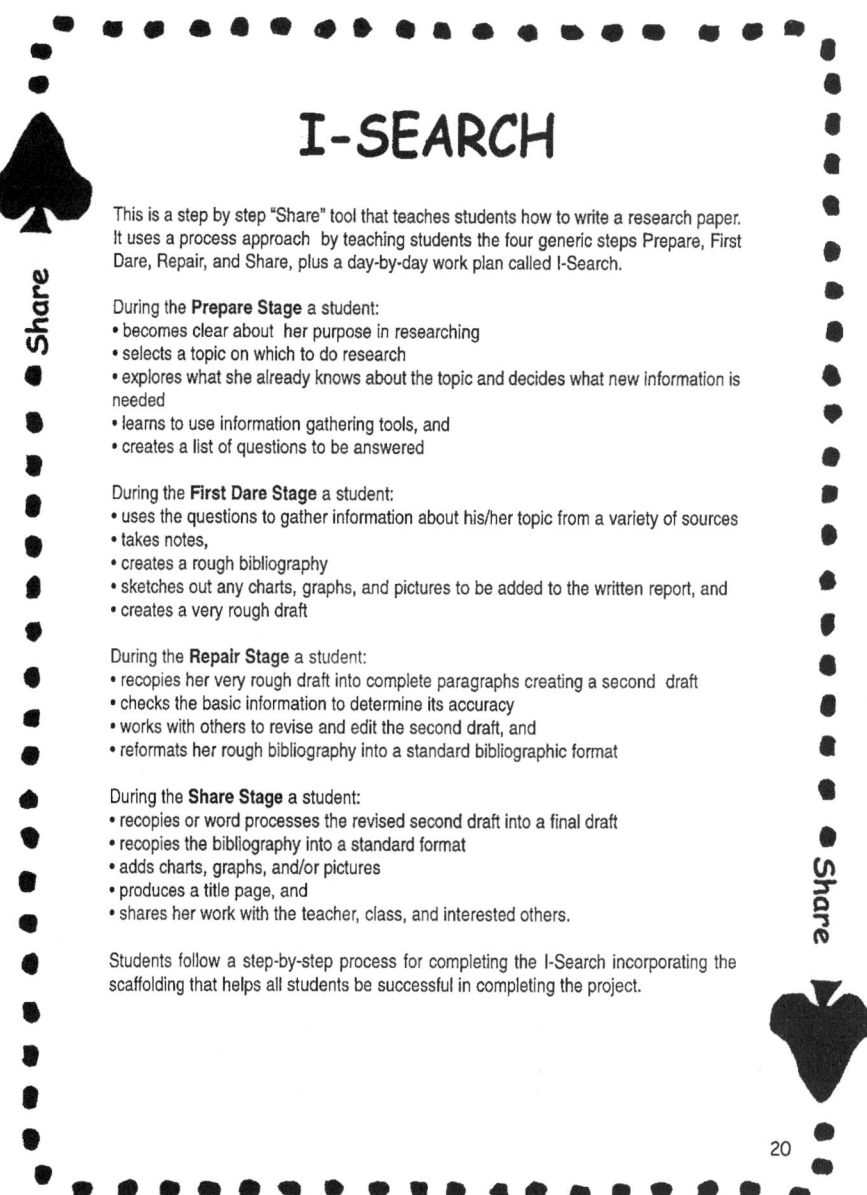

Figure 5.14

I talked to the class about the fact that basic research involves asking and answering questions like these. I also introduced them to the process approach to writing and made a bulletin board display illustrating the steps: (a) Prepare: Prewriting, (b) First Dare: Drafting, (c) Repair: Revising and editing, and (d) Share: Publishing a final draft.

I made a chart to display the steps in I-Search, and I mounted it in the front of the classroom. I worked from Figure 5.14 to create the chart. However, I did not display all the steps at one time. I simply left the chart covered until we had reached a particular stage in the process. Then I would uncover that step and explain it to students. I should note that I gathered information together before class to aid in answering questions, and I modeled using a table of contents and index in locating information. In addition, I invited in experts, as well as viewed videos, to add to the "info in" mix. As these presentations occurred, I would frequently stop and ask the class to help me create notes about the key points.

Those of you who teach in the primary grades will appreciate that we worked together as a group on charts to create all work in arriving at a rough draft and works-cited list. However, to increase the feelings of accomplishment on the part of students, I had fifth graders come to our classroom at the end of the project and assist each student in creating their own final draft and works cited. To make it even more special, the work was placed in a nice folio with a clear cover. Students then created a title page with illustrations added. Needless to say, all were very proud of their work. (I still have that rock tumbler in my garage!)

"Info Out" With Visuals

Enough writing already! Time to change to the visual/graphic/illustrative mode. As great as writing is across subjects and grade levels, we cannot be trapped into using it as the exclusive "Info Out" mode. Some students (and teachers) are more comfortable sharing information through a graphic display, such as a drawing, a collage, a concept web, or a computer slide show. Plus, all learners should be asked, on occasion, to try out this important mode.

The visual mode is most highly regarded in the commercial world. We are well aware of the role of pictures, images, and other graphic representations in advertising. Text (words) is used sparingly and only to support the visuals—very powerful stuff when done well. What Marshall McLuhan wrote decades ago is still true: "The medium is the message."

Monsters Before and After

We will begin with a primary tool that uses drawing to share understanding. It was invented by first-grade teacher Tracy Dabbs at West View School in Burlington, Washington. She read a story to her class about a monster that came to school. As in most literature, the character undergoes some change that affects the plot. To ascertain which kids understood this change, or more accurately, to what *degree* each student understood the content, Tracy provided them with an outline of a monster labeled "Before." Inside the shape, the

The Share Suit: Show What You Are Learning 103

Figure 5.15 The Monster *Before*

students drew a picture to express what they had learned about the monster early in the story. See Tyler's drawing in Figure 5.15.

Next, Tracy distributed another monster worksheet, but she labeled it "After." Notice the change in character that Tyler detected also in Figure 5.15.

This activity reminds us of the Open Mind introduced in chapter 2 (p. 11) and revisited earlier in this chapter. The differences are the change in shape (to match the content) and the provision of two shapes instead of one. Obviously, any teacher can take Tracy's idea and modify it to fit any topic at any grade level. Students will rely on drawing to communicate understanding, with writing serving as a support tool.

We already saw a similar visual/text tool in chapter 3, in Eric Schott's Shakespearean scenes. His high school lit. students illustrated a key action in scenes from *Macbeth,* and then they turned the paper over to write a description of the scene, identifying the importance it has to the play.

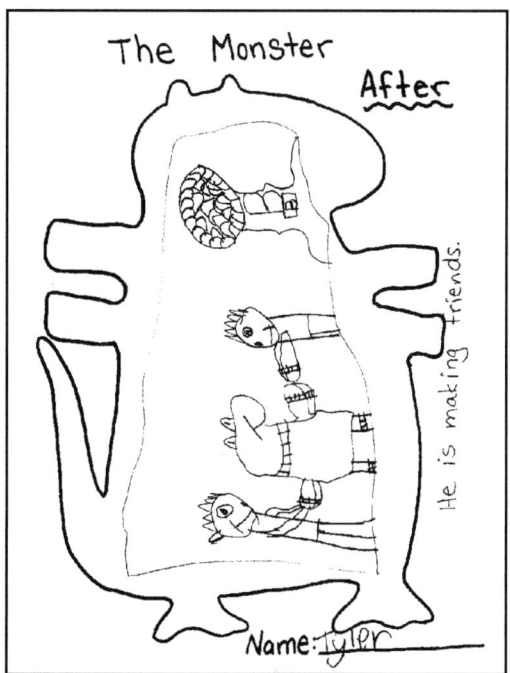

Figure 5.15 The Monster *After (continued)*

Comic Strips and Comic Books

Also in chapter 3, we introduced the First Dare tool "SnapShots." Students make quick sketches while reading to stimulate visualizations of the content. Text also played a supporting role when students wrote brief captions beneath each snapshot.

We can modify this tool into a comic strip. We have used them with students as a motivating tool to share understanding, such as a historical comic strip depicting the sinking of the *Santa Maria*. (See *Great Performances: Creating Classroom-Based Performance Tasks,* Lewin & Shoemaker, pages 26–28, ASCD, 1998.)

Franzi Thompson, fourth-year Spanish teacher at South Eugene High School in our Eugene, Oregon, school district, employed comic strips when teaching Spanish literature. Instead of relying on a quiz for "Info Out" on the short story "El Lago Encantado" ("The Enchanted Lake"), Franzi showed her class how to draw comic strips. See Figure 5.16 for Eli and Rita's outstanding literary comic strip.

Figure 5.16

The time allotment in class depends on the students. In slower-moving classes, Franzi allows one class period to begin and plan (50 minutes) and then 20–30 minutes on two consecutive days to complete the project. It really varies.

To save class time, an option would be to send another blank copy of the comic strip home and instruct the students to do their drawings individually as a homework assignment. They could then bring it to class and paste their section on the whole strip. So, in essence, they could do one planning period, including division of labor and generation of ideas, then take it home and individually draw their parts, and then cut and paste the following day in a half-hour period. In Franzi's class, they would need to write on it in Spanish, of course, so they could do their dialogue boxes in class together first on a separate piece of paper, check them together for errors or perfection, and then write the perfected dialogues on the strip in pen.

A nice extension activity could be a presentation to the class, including what scenes they drew, why they selected them, why they used the colors they did to lend the feeling of the drawing to the viewer, and so forth. As an integrated art lesson, a discussion on the elements of art before activity will provide them with a vocabulary to describe their work, and the students listening to the presentation will also have working knowledge of the same vocabulary and the concepts.

Franzi was pleased with the results. She wrote us:

> Hola, Lorenzo y Bette:
>
> Each student read the same legend but did his own version of the legend as a group art/lit project. I would be thrilled to have you use them, errors and all—progress not perfection.
>
> I have them do the paraphrasing activity "get the gist" first (see chapter 3), and then do the comic strip afterwards.
>
> Even the students in the other Spanish classes in the same room were asking about the story, which is a good sign.
>
> Thanks for all of your hard work; you are improving my teaching and inspiring me.
>
> Franzi

Thanks, Franzi. You are improving our teaching and inspiring us.

The clear advantage to comic strips is the incentive it provides for students to share what they have learned. Comics are fun, they are different from usual schoolwork, and they tap into the visual mode of expression. To facilitate the use of comic strips in class, we have collected a set of "Comic Strip Tips" from teachers. It is posted at http://www.larrylewin.com/Struggling/comicstriptips.htm. So, due to time constraints, comic strips are not used very often. That's okay. We have lots of other tools in our teacher toolkit, including SnapShots, which actually are streamlined comic strips.

Now, if time is not going to limit you, comic strips can be reformatted into comic books. This allows students to go into a more detailed sharing.

Christopher Hudson's students learned about the procedure for passing a law in Congress. To impart this content knowledge, they drew "How a Bill Becomes a Law" comic books. The panels are stapled together to make a booklet instead of glued across a piece of larger paper.

106 Innovative Instruction: A Menu of Teaching Tools for Effective Student Learning

Christopher was pleased with the results. He wrote us, "All in all, I feel that it was successful. The students learned more because they had some fun doing the exercise. The trick is to keep the ideas fresh with students."

Even classic literature does well as a comic. How many of us have read the Classic Comic versions of famous literature? The combination of minimal text with colorful pictures makes comprehension of the basics easier. Like the CliffNotes® versions, the Classic Comics offer a smooth entré to the fuller, richer, weightier literary version.

The Story Diamond

Primary teachers can easily modify the comic strip or comic book into a more doable tool for Grades K–3. Marsha Ruhn at Glide Elementary supplied her third graders with a large piece of white drawing paper with a large diamond in the center. In the diamond, they drew a picture of a key scene from a story they

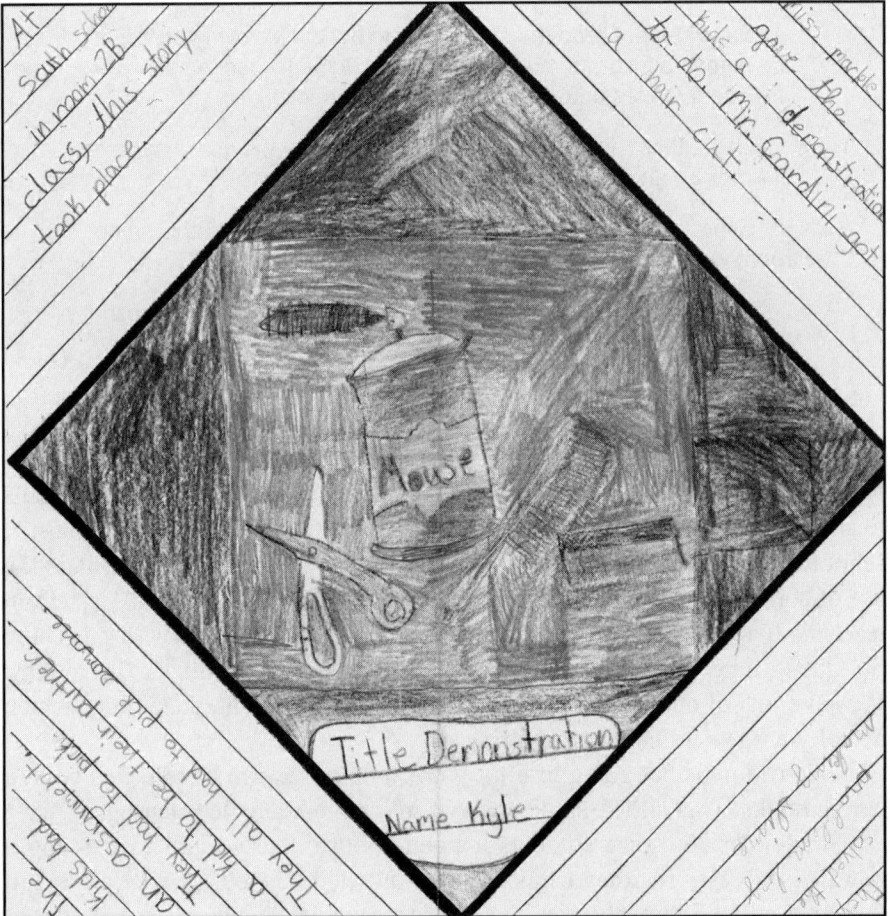

Figure 5.17

had read. In each of the four corners, the students wrote a summary of the elements of fiction (see Figure 5.17). Combining drawing and writing has been a powerful learning tool forever. In order for them to appear interesting and fresh to students, we need to come up with new "looks," as Marsha did.

Invention Illustration

In order to use this visual/graphic/pictorial mode successfully, we must remember to add structure and clear directions to the assignment. For example, Terry Osgerby, in Spirit Lake Middle School, Iowa, provided his seventh graders with a "Help Sheet" as they studied the role of inventions in their social studies class.

> Prepare an illustration on a given invention of your choice. Be sure to include
> 1. Date of the invention's creation
> 2. Specific location of its origin
> 3. Developments leading to need
> 4. Connect it to the 5 themes of geography
>   - Use a pentagon to format the 5 themes
>   - Illustrate each theme as it applies to the invention
>   - Place your illustration of the invention in the center

Additionally, Terry provided his students with an "Invention Rubric," so that they could self-assess their illustrations before he assessed them (see Figure 5.25).

EGOs

Electronic graphic organizers (EGOs) are computer-generated graphic organizers. The advantages of using software to create concept maps, webs, flow charts, clusters, and so forth, are numerous: library of shapes, symbols, and icons; automatic linking of shapes; word processor built-in; ease of editing; and kids' general love of using computers.

More and more teachers are using Inspiration® software with their students to "Info Out" book reports. By switching the mode from a written book report to a visual graphic organizer, she was able to tap into the energy and creativity of students who were either unskilled book review writers or who were sick of doing them.

The information presented by the student is the same in either mode, but the EGO is more inspiring to many students.

A high school special education student in Vicky Ayer's class at South Eugene High School in Oregon, studied the U.S. Constitution and tracked her "Info In" by creating an EGO. For her section on the Supreme Court, she used

Inspiration®'s note feature to post a photo of Justice Ruth Bader-Ginsberg (see Figure 5.18).

Inspiration® software is gaining the attention of teachers and students, due to its ease of use. However, nonelectronic graphic organizers have been used in classrooms for years. Paper and pencils are still a viable choice for sharing content information.

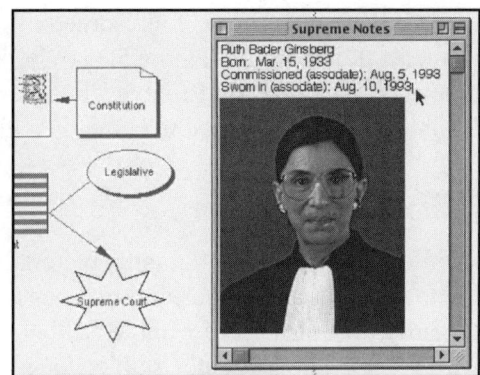

Figure 5.18

"Info Out" by Speaking

The Ancient Greeks used speaking as their primary mode of teaching, learning, and assessing. We would love to use it as well, because of the power of dialogue. One-on-one conferences, debating, and small-group discussing are surely effective ways to engage students in their learning. But reality prevents us from using the oral mode as much as we would like. Class sizes limit our ability to assign formal speeches, one-on-one conferences, and other speaking tools. However, rather than abandoning this mode, we must adjust it to fit into the reality of our classrooms.

Round Robin Minispeeches

Whole-class speeches, as in Oral Book Reports, can take up to a full week of class time. Thirty students times five minutes, plus discussion time, plus transition time between speakers, equals a lot of time. So the Round Robin Minispeeches are a reasonable compromise.

Students present their content information ("Info Out") to a small group of listeners, say 5 or 6 students, instead of standing in front of the whole class (see Amy in Figure 5.19). After the five minute mini-speech, the audience says goodbye to Amy, and rotates to a different location in the classroom and listens to a different speaker present, like Chris or Navin in Figure 5.20. Finally, the group roves to a third location to hear a third minispeech.

Several advantages emerge: (a) Kids get to move from speaker to speaker. While this takes

Figure 5.19 Amy's round robin minispeech

Figure 5.20 Chris' and Navin's round robin minispeeches

up some time, the physical movement is helpful in keeping them fresh for the next speaker, (b) in a small group, each listener is closer to each speaker, which helps focus and attention, (c) for the speakers, many find it less intimidating to speak to a small group than to the large group, and (d) the speakers all get to repeat their minispeeches to different audiences. This is helpful in actually getting good at it.

To save time, not every group of listeners must listen to every minispeech. Say you have six kids scheduled to present on Tuesday, but you only have 20 minutes allotted. Each rotating audience listens to three minispeeches instead of all six. The speakers get to repeat their speech three times, the audiences get to move around and hear three different speeches, and you just completed 1/5 of the speakers (6 out of 30) in 20 minutes, instead of 40 minutes if each speaker addresses the whole class. A reasonable compromise.

Two helpful hints from Dorothy Syfert, teacher at Monroe Middle School, in Eugene, Oregon, who taught us this tool. First, to help the speaker speak intelligently and coherently, a graphic organizer (GO) serving as notes is permitted. Notice that both Amy and Chris in Figures 5.19 and 5.20 are using GOs—Amy's handdrawn and Chris' with Inspiration®.

Second, to help the miniaudiences attend to the speaker, some notetaking device is provided. Notice in Figures 5.19 and 5.20 that the listeners are listening with pencils in their hands, taking notes. Some options are: a blank graphic organizer provided by the speaker to fill in while listening; a set of index cards, one for each speaker, to jot two key points—one comment, and one question; or a minibooklet of stapled sheets of paper, one page for each speech, ending up with a collective booklet. Of course, whichever method is applied, smart instruction would include some time on teaching the students *how to* take notes using the device(s).

The Simulated Trial

Conducting a trial is a thrilling way to engage students in sharing what they have learned. It requires them to go deeper into the content by taking a position and arguing it in the structure of a courtroom.

Judy McFadden's students in Mountain Home, Idaho, studied the Boston Massacre as many U.S. History students do. To "Info Out" their understanding of this important historical event, Judy assigns students to certain roles—Judge, Lawyers for Prosecution and Defense, Witnesses, and British Captain Thomas Preston (the accused). She meets briefly with each character and provides them with a 1/2 sheet listing of key points. It is up to each actor to use the notes and ad-lib in character in the courtroom. She acts as the bailiff who swears in witnesses (placing hand on top of the social studies textbook), and keeps the trial moving along. The other students serve as jury members who vote guilty or innocent with evidence cited. If time allows, a new set of students can act out the trial.

The Boston Massacre is perfect, of course, for this tool. But other topics also fit into the Simulated Trial. Other historical events, scientific discoveries, and the actions of characters in literature can be "put on trial."

The Internet's World Wide Web offers lots of Web site resources on mock trials. For a sampling of Web sites, see Appendix.

Reader's Theater

Merging the reading of literature ("Info In") with oral presentation of that literature ("Info Out") is Reader's Theater. According to Aaron Shepard (http://www.aaronshep.com/rt/whatis.html), a major popularizer of this tool:

> Reader's theater was developed as a convenient and effective means to present literary works in dramatic form. This is still its primary use, though many scripts now published are original dramatic works rather than literary adaptations. . . . Kids love to do it, and they give it their all—more so because it's a team effort, and they don't want to let down their friends! And if the script is based on an available book, they of course want to read it. What's more, reader's theater is a simple activity for the teacher, since it requires no setup apart from the reproduction of scripts.
>
> Reader's theater is minimal theater in support of literature and reading. There are many styles of reader's theater, but nearly all share these traits:
>
> - No full memorization. Scripts are held during performance.
> - No full costume. If used at all, costumes are partial and suggestive, or neutral and uniform.
> - No full stage sets. If used at all, sets are simple and suggestive.
> - Narration provides the framework for dramatic action.

We encourage you, if you try Reader's Theater with your students, to partner your students up on reading the same parts. They can practice together, though no one person stands out as either a good reader or poor reader. It also gives students a chance to practice with each other, modeling both improvement in prosody and rate.

The Literature Play

Primary students also love to act out scenes from a story they are reading (or listening to) because it brings the characters to life. No need for a simulated trial. Students are assigned to play characters, they meet with the teacher to identify key points, and then they act out a scene from the book in character. I (Larry) still remember my second-grade role in the classic *Caps for Sale*, not knowing who the story was written by.

We searched the Internet for the author and illustrator. Esphyr Slobodkina (New York: Harper & Row, 1985). We also found some primary teachers who shared their ideas.

Corinne Levine, Grade 1 teacher at Stony Point Elementary School, New York, knows that children love to mimic the monkeys and act out the story. She integrates some mathematics with studying combinations of ten, and also adds writing: The children write a new ending for the story based on the prompt, "What happened in the next town the peddler visited?" (http://www.eduplace.com/tview/tviews/c/capsforsale.html)

On the Teach.net posting board, we found this idea:

> Read the story several times to familiarize the children with it.
>
> Talk about peddlers and how they sell their wares.
>
> Dramatize the story. Decorate painters caps in class and then use those. The peddler can wear a lady's blazer and you could make monkey masks, but they aren't necessary. The children have no problem being monkeys! The teacher will probably need to be the narrator. (http://teachers.net/lessons/posts/527.html)

When using any of the above oral tools, a teacher could opt to assess the speaking abilities of the students. Of course, a list of the key ingredients to successful speaking would be essential.

Eddie Willing, in Monitor School in Mt. Angel, Oregon, took his state's standards for speaking and created a first-page "Speech Checklist" to direct his students' attention to improving their speaking by meeting the four required traits: Ideas/Content, Organization, Language, and Delivery (see Figure 5.21). This teacher-made rubric nicely bridges us to our final section.

```
Name: _____

Grade: _____          Date: _____

Type: _____    Time: _____

Subject: _____
```

Ideas and Content: _____

○ clear main idea and purpose   ○ did not meet time requirement
○ solid details   ○ main idea identified, not strong
○ adapts info to audience and purpose   ○ details unclear, underdeveloped
                                        ○ problems adapting info to audience and purpose

Organization: _____

                                        ○ did not meet time requirement
○ introduction smooth   ○ beginning underdeveloped
○ organized thoughts, message clear   ○ thoughts sometimes unclear
○ details fit   ○ details confuse listener
○ good conclusion   ○ conclusion too short

Language: _____

○ message is stated clearly   ○ message stated, but uses ordinary language
○ slang or technical language used properly   ○ slang or technical language used incorrectly
○ use of words and grammar mostly correct   ○ mistakes in grammar distract

Delivery: _____

○ frequent eye contact   ○ little eye contact - reads notes
○ word usage clear and correct   ○ several mistakes in word usage
○ rate and volume satisfactory   ○ rate and volume - too fast, too soft
○ uses gestures well   ○ gestures distract from message

Figure 5.21 Speech checklist

Sharing as Assessment

The intention of the "Share" stage of the learning process is to provide learners with a venue for revealing their understandings of newly learned content. Second, the "Share" stage is used for adding incentive to learn. It acts as a motivating payoff for investing time and energy into "preparing, first daring, and repairing." New, different, and engaging tools like Snapshots, postcards, and round robin minispeeches not only urge students to disclose their understanding but also to put forth their best effort in doing so.

A third role that the "Share" stage can play in a classroom is the assessment role. Obviously, when students "Info Out," their teachers take notice. And we take special notice by evaluating their outputs systematically. This is known as classroom-based assessment.

Two key factors must be present to use student work as assessments. First, students need to know that their work will be assessed. And they need to know exactly what aspects of the work are targeted for evaluation. Is it the *product* that they will be creating, or is it the *process* they will follow to create the product?

Second, students must understand how they will be assessed. What is the scoring scale the teacher will be using to evaluate?

For example, when Jan Ross, a middle-school teacher in Colorado Springs, assigned student comics, she created a 4-point rubric for assessing them. Rubrics accomplish both the key ingredients for employing the "Share" stage as assessment: They reveal both the targets (traits) and the scoring scale (4-point). Jan selected four key traits of quality comic strips and listed them along the left side. She then described for her students the degrees of proficiency across the top columns. Jan opted to assess her students' proficiency on the final product (see Figure 5.22).

COMIC STRIP	4	3	2	1
CHARACTERS	Included and identified <u>all</u> of the required characters.	Included and identified <u>most</u> of the required characters.	Included and/or identified only some of the required characters.	Only one or two characters identified or included.
SEQUENCE OF EVENTS	All events are in correct order and show a clear sequence which flows smoothly.	Most events are included but may be out of sequence or does not flow smoothly.	There are several events missing or out of order.	The important events are missing. Big gaps in sequence.
UNDERSTANDING OF EVENTS	Shows exceptional understanding of why the events occurred & how the characters were affected by the events.	Shows some understanding of why events occurred and how the characters were affected.	Shows little understanding of why events occurred and how the characters were affected.	Shows no understanding of cause and effect of events.
APPEARANCE & PRESENTATION	Cartoon panels used (outlined). Talking and/or thought bubbles and/or story line narrative boxes used effectively. All words spelled correctly.	Cartoon panels used (and outlined). Bubbles & narrative boxes used but are not easy to read (too small). Most words spelled correctly.	Cartoon panels used. Some words are misspelled. Bubbles & narrative boxes are too few and difficult to read.	Cartoon panels not outlined. No bubbles or narrative boxes used. Spelling is poor.

Figure 5.22 Comic strip assessment rubric

Susan Strano assigned Colonial American news articles to her class. She evaluated student proficiency at each stage of the writing *process*: Prepare, First Dare, Repair, and Share, by using a rubric with a 6-point scoring scale that she picked up from a workshop and shared it with us. Naturally, she provided her students with the rubric at the early stage of the writing assignment, so that the young journalists knew exactly what she expected them to do (see Figure 5.23).

Directions: When you have completed your project, use the questions below to evaluate your performance.
Use a scale of 1 to 6 to score each aspect of your performance
1 being the lowest and 6 being the best.

Use the following information to choose your scores.
6 — Student meets ALL criteria listed for this category
5 — Student meets MOST of the criteria listed for this category
4 — Student meets MANY of the criteria listed for this category
3 — Student meets 1 or 2 of the criteria, but is weak in several
2 — Student fails to meet most of the criteria listed for category
1 — Student fails to meet any of the criteria listed for category

Student Self-Evaluation   *Teacher Evaluation*
6 5 4 3 2 1   *Stage #1 PREPARE*   6 5 4 3 2 1

1. *Did you follow directions regarding research steps?*
2. *Did you use/ document a wide variety of sources?*
3. *Did you carefully pre-plan your project format?*
4. *Does your project reflect new information?*

Stage #2 FIRST DARE

5. *Did you include all assigned components?*
6. *Did you include assigned newspaper components?*
7. *Did you place stories, etc. in appropriate sections?*
8. *Did you make sure your information is accurate?*

6 5 4 3 2 1   *Stage #3 REPAIR*   6 5 4 3 2 1

9. *Did you correct all mechanical mistakes such as spelling and grammar?*
10. *Is all information relevant to your assigned topic?*
11. *Did you carefully copy read your final product?*
12. *Did you include rough copy, etc. in your portfolio?*

Stage #4 SHARE

13. *Did you produce a computer AND printed copy?*
14. *How would you rate your group's ORAL sharing?*
15. *Does your final project reflect a theme?*
16. *How would you rate your group's performance?*
17. *How would you rate YOUR overall performance?*

_____ *Self Evaluation Total*   *Teacher Evaluation Total* _____

TOTAL POSSIBLE: 102 points
Additional Student Comments: *Additional Teacher/Evaluator Comments:*

Figure 5.23 Colonial newspaper evaluation

Likewise, to provide feedback on her students' writing, Oregon high school teacher Eliza Sher used a scoring device called the *ChecBric* to assess the book reviews. ChecBrics are like rubrics, but they also provide students with checklists. See Figure 5.24 for the two-columned formatting: left column checklist for students, right column rubric for the teacher. Notice that this ChecBric evaluates the *product*, the book review.

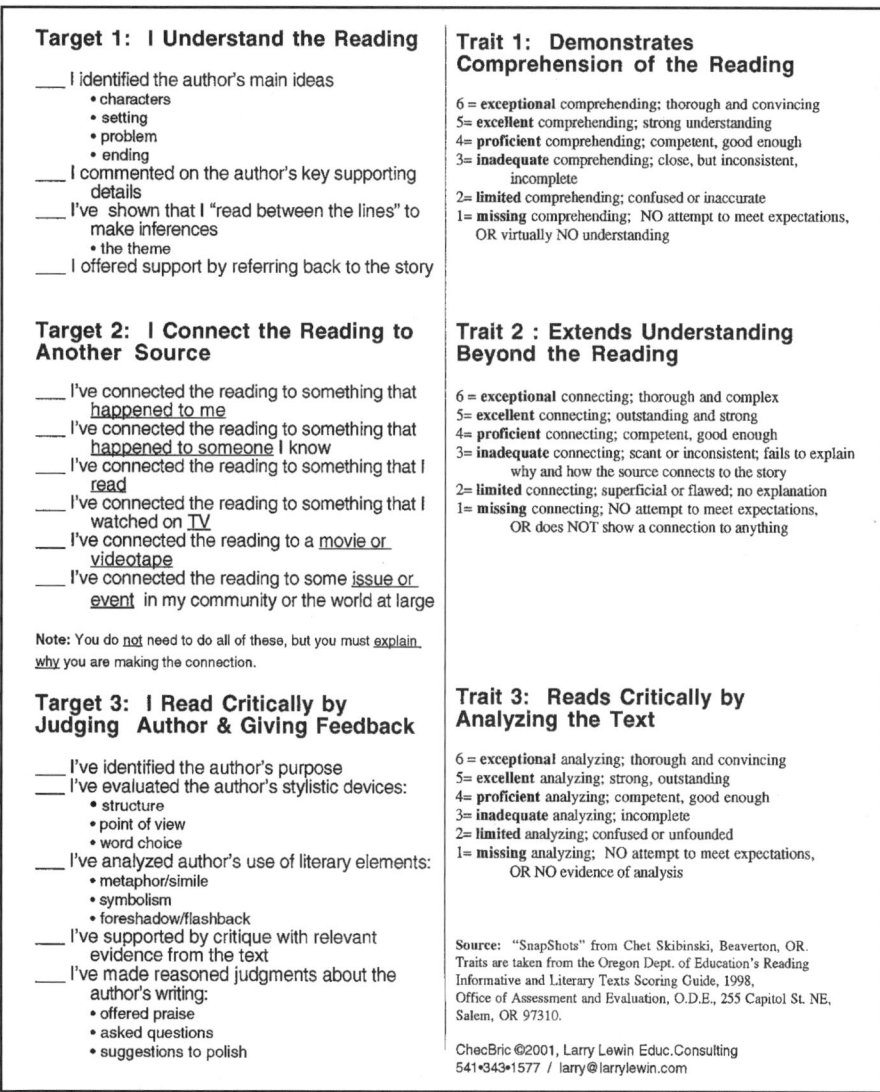

Figure 5-24 Book review ChecBric

We prefer ChecBrics because they are more student friendly. While students can be trained to read and understand rubrics, they typically are written in teacher language and provide way too much text for most students to wrestle with. Checklists are easier for students to deal with: shorter text, easy words, and a blank line to check off when complete. Since both are helpful for assessment, we created the ChecBric, a hybrid that makes use of the best of both devices (see Figure 5.24).

Terry Osgerby's "Invention Illustration" was described earlier as a Share tool. To make this into an assessment, Terry provided his students with an "Invention Rubric" so that they could self-assess their illustrations before he assessed them (see Figure 5.25).

SOCIAL STUDIES CHAPTER 1: LESSON 3				NAME_____ CLASS____	
Self	Teacher	Topic	5/4 points	3 points	2/1 points
----- 5	----- 5	A. Show how an invention creates change	Shows 2 or more developments of an invention	Shows one development about an invention	Shows little or no development

----- 	
5
	----- 	
	5
		B. Identify the themes of geography
		  1. Location
		  2. Place
		  3. Change
		  4. Movement
		  5. Region
			Illustrates 4-5 themes very well, using clear, creative & attractive drawings or pictures	Illustrates only 3 themes well, or uses good drawings that are attractive but could use more creativity	Illustrates only 1-2 themes or uses unclear or unattractive pictures

----- 5	----- 5	C. Construct an illustration around a pentagon	Excellent use of color, value, shape & possibly some texture or spacing	Good use of color, shape & value or some texture or spacing	Little color was used, with some spacing and little value
----- 5	----- 5	D. Label the sides of the pentagon	Labels of the 5 themes were attractive & neatly positioned	Label of the 5 themes were in the proper place & easy to read	Labels were unclear or untidy
----- 5	----- 5	E. Make your best effort	Good to excellent effort was made to be creative and original	Illustrations were mostly original with some good use of creativity	Lack of originality, and little effort made to be creative
----- 25	----- 25				

Figure 5.25 Invention rubric

Conclusion

Teaching and learning are linked through "sharing." Teachers teach and kids learn. But this simple equation is not so simple in a real classroom. In fact, it represents a complex, intriguing, and even mystifying exchange.

As teachers, we need to somehow measure that exchange so that the students know what they have learned and how well they have learned it—cashing in their chips, if you will. As their teachers, we also need to know so that we can assess our teaching and their learning.

Sharing comes in many different formats. We have looked at the written mode, the visual mode, and the oral mode. For each mode, we have provided many different tools that are designed to motivate, inspire, and "incentivise" learners.

Sharing should be a big deal in school. It should be fun, engaging, and important. By adding these new tools to our toolkits, we can make this stage work for us . . . and for our students.

Figure 5.26 Teaching devices introduced in chapter 5

Endnotes

1. Peddiwell, J. A. (1937). *The saber-tooth curriculum.* New York: McGraw-Hill.

2. You can find a description of this tool along with many others in his excellent book, *After the end: Teaching and learning creative revision.* It was published by Heinemann Publishers, Portsmouth, New Hampshire, in 1993.

CHAPTER
SIX

What Works

"Hold All the Aces"

An ace is the highest card in each suit. To hold all the aces gives one a distinct advantage. When it comes to evaluating our instruction, our students hold all the aces—they have the advantage. Because learning is personal, we teachers have to work hard to get students to show their hands—to reveal their learning.

Betty's Story

As a child, I had many adventures on our family farm. One of my favorite summer experiences involved carving large, overgrown cucumbers into floating cucumber boats. Yup! You can actually float a cucumber on water. "How does it work?," you're asking.

First, you drop the cucumber in water and let it rise, to determine the side that naturally floats above the surface. Mark that area above the water with a pencil. Remove the cucumber from the water and carve out its cavity respecting the pencil-delineated line. You can then spend hours decorating your boat and floating it in small pools of water.

You may be asking, "What does this have to do with evaluating the effectiveness of one's teaching?" Well, that turns out to be one interesting story. One early fall day, a friend of mine shared that he had so neglected his garden, that his cucumber patch was overtaking everything. He acknowledged that he had 40 or 50 very large cucumbers on the vine, all too large to be tasty. I immediately flashed back to numerous childhood memories of cucumber boats. I suggested to my teaching partner, Mary, that this may be a great opportunity for us—a "teachable" moment, as it were. We were both planning to teach the math chapter on units of measurement with our first graders. I suggested that we could develop various activities to practice multiple ways of measuring an object and then, for fun, have students carve the cukes into boats. Mary, another farm girl, was in! We set about gathering newspapers, carving tools, and several child-sized wading pools in which to float the boats. As we made our plans for maximizing this teachable moment, we became more and more excited at the possibilities.

A few days later, my gardener friend delivered the cucumbers, each student was given his own, and we set to work. We estimated and predicted, measured and weighed, and assigned awards for various cucumber features. During the teaching experience, I knew intuitively that things were going well. Students were engaged throughout the activities. The hands-on lessons brought forth insightful, in-depth descriptions of measurement concepts. Both Mary and I were thrilled. We even used the experience to explore beginning concepts of buoyancy with students.

All of our students then carved out the most creative vessels. Some students carved out covered areas, and some attached homemade umbrellas to shade the imaginary passengers. During recess, both classes headed outside to float their boats in one of the various wading pools we had borrowed.

As it happened, both Mary and I were on playground duty that day. As we took our 360°-turnabout, scanning the horizon for any untoward activities, we talked about how successful the experience had been. Some students weren't quite ready to float their creations, so we said that kids could finish up over the next couple of minutes and head outside. Unbeknownst to us, a couple of our students (twin brothers, one assigned to each of our rooms) reentered my classroom. As they crossed the threshold, one cucumber slipped and fell from a hand. Cucumber pulp flew up and away in such an interesting pattern. Soon, both boys were caught up in the joy of smashing cucumbers all over the inside of both classrooms. The more they smashed, the more fun they had, and the more decorative the walls and ceilings became.

We returned from recess absolutely stunned from all the carnage. I'll never forget the look of the custodian standing in the hallway between our two rooms, shaking his head in despair and disbelief. Years later, some colleagues joked that the smashing cucumber crew was the precursor to the famous rock band the *Smashing Pumpkins*. And even years later, we were still scraping cuke seeds from the walls, carpet, and desks.

The point in all this pulp is: Were the lessons successful? For whom? Was this a teachable moment, or did we get ourselves into a real "pickle?" Well, it depends on the way you look at it.

Students Hold All the Aces on the Effectiveness of Your Instruction

As educators, we have a fundamental responsibility to ask ourselves, "What evidence do I have that what I do contributes to student *growth* and *achievement*?" We chose these two words carefully. In these days of standards and assessments, sometimes we see student growth as two dimensional: (a) can the student read, write, compute, and problem solve to a high level of sophistication (procedural knowledge), and (b) does the student comprehend key facts, concepts, and generalizations in particular subject areas (declarative knowledge)? This is what some mean by *achievement*. However, achievement is not the only growth we are interested in as teachers. We want students to *grow into* the roles of responsible citizens, workers, and parents, among others. As teachers, we need to examine our approaches to instruction as if the tools we use are designed to be three-dimensional. That is, are the teaching tools we are using contributing to student mastery of both procedural knowledge and declarative knowledge, as well as contributing to *growth* in conditional knowledge—those metacognitive strategies involving synthesis and application so important to the life and career roles in successful and fulfilling adult living.

In this chapter, we intend to focus on ways in which you can *pervasively* evaluate what you do to determine the effectiveness of your methodology in a three-dimensional way. And let's face it. Students hold all the "aces" when it comes to evaluating the effectiveness of your instruction. They are your clients, and what they are getting out of the instruction you provide is a personal affair. Your goal as their teacher is to pick up as many clues as you can from what they do reveal about how things are going for them. What are aces? ACES are clues that students give you to let you know how everything is going. They include

- **Academic performance clues**—mini, midi, and maxi products produced throughout the unit that reveal student thinking
- **Conduct clues**—behavioral clues that indicate a lack of understanding and/or engagement
- **Expressive clues**—expressions of confusion in writing or speaking
- **Sensing clues**—in-your-gut intuition about a student performance

Figure 6.1 graphically represents the ACES concept in a chart format that Betty uses when she trains teachers.

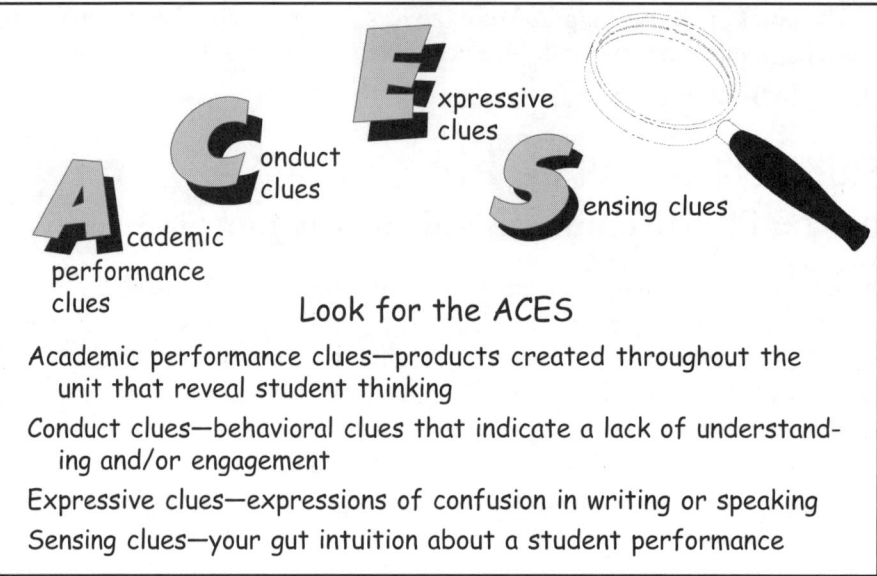

Figure 6.1 ACES chart for teachers

Before we discuss the ACES in more detail, we want to make one critical point, then take you on a short scenic "theory stop" about teaching and learning and end with another critical point about attending to your pedagogy. These points will help you structure your instruction in such a way as to nudge students to play more of their ACES.

Rule #1: Pay Attention All the Way!

First, let us introduce you to our #1, super-duper, golden rule of evaluating one's instruction: PAY ATTENTION ALL THE WAY! When you use the process approach (Prepare, First Dare, Repair, and Share) in your own planning and teaching, you must pay attention to the effectiveness of your teaching from the beginning: as you Prepare—plan your instruction; as you First Dare—launch the unit of instruction with students; as you Repair—continue the instruction, making adjustments as necessary; and as you Share—wrap it all up and reflect on the unit as a whole. "What does this mean in actual practice?," you may be asking. Let us explain.

A "Prepare" Theory Stop: Planning for Instruction

Are there things that you can do to increase student acquisition of meaningful knowledge before you ever begin teaching the unit? We answer with a resounding "Yes!" Many times we have observed and/or experienced for ourselves the failure of a lesson or unit based on poor and inadequate "all the way" planning. The infamous cucumber fete may have been more successful had we planned more carefully about how to "wrap it up" and what to do with students who needed more time or desired "further investigation."

Researchers have contributed substantially to our knowledge about human cognition, about how people learn, and about what constitutes effective teaching methodology. They are continuing to study what learning is, where and how it happens best, and how it can be improved. We are particularly impressed with the work being done at Harvard University and the University of Pittsburgh Learning and Research Development Center.[1]

We started out to create our own Letterman (David Letterman is a late night talk show host)—we mean Shoe'nLewinman—Top Ten List of key findings from the teaching and learning research that should be incorporated into unit planning as one prepares for teaching. The Shoe'nLewinman List eventually settled into a list of 13 key ideas. We extrapolated them from a large body of research conducted on teaching and learning. See Figure 6.2 for our list.

---

1. Learning is shaped by the learner's prior knowledge.
    a. What one already knows or thinks he knows about the concepts is a major influence in acquiring new understandings.
    b. It is important for teachers to delve into and understand student's current conceptions before introducing new material.
2. Learning is largely a social process.
    a. Learners learn in collaboration with others.
    b. Teachers should invite dialogue—an exchange of ideas about the topic at hand. These discussions should include reason and rebuttal.
3. Learning occurs in a climate of trust and mutual respect.
    a. Learners thrive in safe and supportive environments where trusting relationships are established.
    b. When empowering language and behavior are present, learning increases.
4. Learning is closely tied to particular situations.
    a. We create knowledge as we go. It is crafted and adapted to the situations in which we find ourselves.
    b. The transfer of knowledge from one setting to another does not occur easily.
    c. Teachers need to create meaningful, "real world" contexts for learning.
5. Learning involves the use of numerous strategies.
    a. Competent people use lots of strategies to accomplish goals.
    b. Useful strategies can and should be taught.
    c. The ability to articulate one's active mental processing (thinking about one's thinking—what strategies to use) is critical to learning.
6. Learning involves the production of authentic products.
    a. When students apply what they are learning in demonstrations that encompass a range from short and specific to lengthy and substantive, they paint a picture of their overall growth and achievement.
    b. Student products should have value to someone outside the classroom—that is, to a larger audience than just the teacher.

Figure 6.2 The Shoe'nLewinman top ten list of keyfindings from the teaching and learning research

7. Learning is self-directed.
    a. When the learner's interest is aroused, when one's needs are met, the most significant learning occurs.
    b. Students learn best when they are actively engaged in the planning, monitoring, and directing of their own learning.
8. Teachers acknowledge that sustained and directed effort can yield high achievement for all.
    a. An effort-based classroom challenges the notion that aptitude determines student achievement and replaces it with the notion that all students, when expertly taught a rigorous curriculum, can achieve.
    b. Teachers send the message that effort is expected and that great things can be accomplished through sustained effort.
9. Teachers define explicitly what we expect students to learn.
    a. Learning outcomes must be explicitly defined and articulated to students if they are expected to meet them.
    b. Models of work that meet standards are publicly displayed and students participate in evaluating their own work.
10. Teachers incorporate opportunities into their routines to regularly recognize student accomplishments.
    a. Acknowledging and celebrating authentic accomplishment is effective in motivating students to put forth and sustain high levels of effort.
    b. Progress points should be identified so that all students, regardless of their entry level, can experience success.
11. Teachers use fair and credible evaluations.
    a. Students are allowed to prepare for evaluations, and their work is graded against clearly articulated standards.
    b. Parents, employers, and other community members see evaluations as credible.
12. Teachers embrace both an academically rigorous curriculum and a thinking curriculum.
    a. Learners use both their declarative knowledge (facts, concepts, and generalizations) and their procedural knowledge (skills, strategies, and processes) as tools to learn more.
    b. Strong units of study incorporate both the "how" of learning (key processes, strategies, and skills) with the "what" of learning (key content knowledge).
13. Teachers encourage substantive and meaningful talk about the concepts being studied.
    a. Talking with others about ideas and work is fundamental to learning.
    b. This talking must be accurate and relevant to the topic and must respond to and further develop what others in the group have said.

Figure 6.2   The Shoe'nLewinman top ten list of key findings from the teaching and learning research (*continued*)

Rule #2: Incorporate Best Practices Into Your Plans at the Prepare Stage

We use these principles to analyze the quality of our teaching as we prepare. Figure 6.3 provides the reader with a checklist that can be used to review and improve the instructional plans in the Prepare stage.

Successful Teaching and Learning Traits:	Questions to Ask Myself as I Plan and Teach:	AH*	NA*
Learning is shaped by the learner's prior knowledge.	Have I built in an opportunity up front for students to tap their prior knowledge about the concept(s)?	??	
Learning is largely a social process.	Have I built in enough hands-on activities with opportunities for teamwork in the unit?	??	
Learning occurs in a climate of trust and mutual respect.	Do I have a plan for giving verbal and nonverbal feedback, particularly when I am frustrated with the class?	??	
Learning is closely tied to particular situations.	Have I provided a meaningful context for learning so that real-life application can occur?	??	
Learning involves the use of numerous strategies.	Have I identified those learning strategies that need to be taught explicitly, and have I developed a plan to teach them?	??	
Learning involves the production of authentic products.	Do I provide a number of opportunities throughout the unit for students to show what they are currently thinking and learning?	??	
Learning must be self-directed.	What opportunities have I built into the unit for student choice and pursuit of interests?	??	
Teachers acknowledge that sustained and directed effort can yield high achievement for all.	Have I embedded messages into the unit that encourage focused and sustained effort?	??	
Teacher define explicitly what we expect students to learn.	Am I clear about what students are to learn, and have I developed explicit plans for making the expectations clear to students?	??	
Teachers regularly recognize students' accomplishments.	Regardless of the entering student performance levels, have I built in opportunities to recognize individual student growth?	??	
Teachers use fair and credible evaluations.	Have I incorporated fair methods of evaluating student work into the unit and provided anchors of excellent work?	??	
Teachers embrace both an academically rigorous curriculum and a thinking curriculum.	Is the unit organized around major concepts, and does it incorporate the teaching of higher order thinking skills?	??	
Teachers encourage substantive and meaningful talk about the concepts being studied.	Have I built in enough opportunities for extended and substantive talk about the concepts being taught?	??	

* AH, I did well. It is Already Here in my plans.   NA, I forgot to plan for this. I Need to Add it.

Figure 6.3   Planning for instruction checklist

So, one way to pay attention all the way is to analyze your plans before you start teaching, to beef up the lessons by matching activities with the key learning principles listed above. If you take the time to do this, we bet the house that students will:

- be more engaged in the process;
- take more ownership in their work;
- produce better products;
- be more thoughtful in reflecting on their work; and
- construct more meaning around the concepts you are teaching.

Rule #3: Keep a Pedagogiofolio

Another way to pay attention all the way is to keep what we call a *pedagogiofolio*. What is a pedagogiofolio? A pedagogiofolio is for teachers what a working folder/portfolio is to students. It is the folder in which you keep track of your pedagogy—including anecdotal notes, your plans, examples of student work, and reflections on the unit as you go. You can include anything in it that will help you evaluate your instruction as well as give you clues as to student comprehension and achievement.

We must admit that keeping a pedagogiofolio is a difficult thing to do. You get busy with so many other things that it is hard to carve out the time to maintain one. However, if you will take the time to do this, you won't regret it. The benefits of keeping a pedagogiofolio include:

1. Important data about your instruction is located in one place.
2. Having the folio available encourages you to write stuff down as it happens, which in turn makes you more reflective about your teaching.
3. The captured data provides information from which you can make adjustments/improvements in your instruction as you go.
4. The folio helps you attend to who it is in class that is getting the attention and who it is who needs to get attention.

We have used those expanding wallet folios that close with a rubber band around the flap. Bette likes the legal size ones, as she can fit in odd-shaped papers. Plus, they are handy to carry home—not that any of us have to work at home on school stuff!

One good idea we have for keeping anecdotal records is one we described in our book, *Great Performances*.[2] Our friend, colleague, and master math teacher, Judi Johnson, suggests that you photocopy the names of each of your students on a sheet of adhesive address labels, creating a label for each student. Keep this list on a clipboard. As you observe individual students and discuss their work with them, jot down quick notes about the exchanges on the appropriate label. At the end of each day, peel off the labels on which you have recorded data and include these in your pedagogiofolio. The following day, scan the mailing label list. The sheet will list all students for whom you have not had exchanges. Target those students that day.

Rule #4: Pay Attention to ACES

Astute teachers pick up on all kinds of clues from students about how things are going throughout the First Dare, Repair, and Share stages. As we said earlier, teachers pick up on **A**cademic performance clues—mini, midi, and maxi products produced throughout the unit that reveal student thinking; **C**onduct clues—behavioral clues that indicate a lack of understanding and/or engagement; **E**xpressive clues—expressions of confusion in writing or speaking; and **S**ensing clues—in-your-gut intuition about a student performance.

For now, let's set aside the **A** in ACES. We will end up with a discussion of **A**cademic performance clues. What about **C**onduct clues, **E**xpressive clues, and **S**ensing clues?

CONDUCT CLUES

We all recognize student **C**onduct clues when the lesson/unit is not going well. They include

- looking down, refusing to maintain eye contact;
- off-task behavior, such as passing notes, talking, moving around the room;
- inattentiveness, daydreaming, (may include doodling);
- quizzical, puzzling looks;
- popping off with silly, inappropriate comments;
- burying book or note just inside desk and peering in frequently to read;
- coughing, blowing nose, wiping eyes;
- slouching in chair or head on desk;
- being tardy or absent;
- and Betty's all time favorite—snoring.

And we all recognize the related behaviors of our colleagues and ourselves:

- laying one's head on one's desk;
- shaking one's head and weeping;
- raising one's voice;

- taking aspirin; and
- pondering retirement.

Don't be misled, however. Sometimes what you see is not what you are actually getting. Here is a story to elaborate.

I (Betty) have participated in a number of clinical supervision experiences coaching new teachers. As a part of the supervision cycle, I along with two or three colleagues, would systematically observe the instruction in first-year teachers' classrooms. We would meet early in the day with the teacher to go over the lesson plans. Each teacher was asked to identify the kind of data that they wanted us to collect as we observed. We then observed in the classroom for about 30 minutes and concluded the cycle with a debrief of the observation.

I vividly remember one day observing a well-ordered classroom at one of our elementary schools. The class of fourth graders was attentive and responsive to the teacher, who had asked us to observe at-task behaviors. As we stood to leave the classroom, one student slipped up to me and asked, "Did we earn the candy bar?"

EXPRESSIVE CLUES

We all recognize classic written or verbal expressions of lack of understanding. Here are some classic clues that we have heard.

teacher: What do we call the scientific study of the universe?
student: The study of the planets and the stars is called "astrology."

teacher: What significant event in European history occurred in the year 1066?
student: The "Mormon" conquest.

teacher: Be sure and bring your Keds® for gym class.
student: My mom says that we can't afford Keds. Will K-Mart® tennis shoes be okay?

teacher: What do you know about the U. S. Courts?
student: Serena and Venus Williams are tops!

teacher: (Toward the end of the year, when meeting a student who lived next door in the driveway) Hi, Mark!
student: You know, you look just like my P.E. teacher.

teacher: Mark, I *am* your P.E. teacher.
student: You are?

Then there is the straightforward types of expression including:

student: I don't understand.
student: I don't know what to do.

student:	What did you say?
student:	What are you? Crazy?
student:	I don't get it.
student:	I *still* don't get it.
student:	What am I supposed to do now?
student:	Teacher, Teacher, Teacher!

SENSING CLUES

We don't want to sound too "woo-woo" here, but we want to reinforce that good teachers pick up on what we call "intuitive" clues. An intuitive clue is a feeling you have in your stomach—a gut feeling. It's a glimpse at something behind the gaze or the talk. It is something you just sense about a student and her connection to the instruction.

Here is a poignant example from Betty's teaching. A number of years ago, a new student came into my classroom in late February. He had just moved to Eugene from a small southern Oregon coastal town that he consistently referred to as "California." His new home was just two houses down the block from our playground.

In class, he seemed anxious and withdrawn for over two weeks. However, many first graders coming into a new situation would behave in a similar fashion, and so I thought I would wait and see if he became more comfortable in class as he settled in and made friends. There was just something about him—something that I sensed that made him seem so vulnerable.

We had a local poet come into our classroom to work with students on a poetry unit I was teaching. When asked to write a simile starting with the prompt, "I am like . . .", he seemed lost in a dream world, away from the class, somewhere in his mind. That evening, when reading over student responses, I came across his statement, "I am like a ship sinking off the coast of California." I thought to myself that I needed to follow-up on this. The following day, before I had a chance to speak with him and while all the kinders and first graders were on morning recess, his dad came out of the house brandishing a rifle and attempted suicide on the front lawn.

When one picks up an intuitive clue, what should one do? Follow up on it! Get the student off to the side and talk. Don't confront them in front of the whole group. Most of us do not like to be put on the spot in front of others. Don't pressure them to talk, but do make clear that you are available if they need help. Enough said about paying attention to your own internal intuition. If your school or district has a counseling team, engage it. And get some training in how to work with students who disclose abusive situations to you.

Back to Academic Clues

When evaluating the effectiveness of your instruction in relation to the Academic performance clues, you need to pay attention to both the products students produce as well as the process they are using to produce the products. This leads us to our fifth rule.

Rule #5: Evaluate Process, Product, and Metacognition

In a standards-based system, a lot of emphasis is placed on getting students to produce great products. We agree that this is important. But, when evaluating student work, you will want to collect evidence relating to both the products that students are producing throughout the unit as well as the processes they are using. Obviously faulty and/or inadequate procedures can lead to the production of faulty, inadequate products. When developing student-friendly scoring guides for use in our district's elementary schools, we deliberately incorporated both process and product into them (see Figures 6.4 and 6.5).

Name:			Date:		
Understands Concepts	Technical Quality	Reflects Creative Thinking	Uses the Process Approach		Displays or Performs the Composition
I understand and use key concepts from the art form in which I am composing.	I apply technical skills appropriate to the artistic form.	I come up with imaginative and inventive ideas.	I come up with a lot of ideas for my composition, then create a design, a model, or draft, revise my draft and produce a final product or performance.		I display or perform my composition.
• I know the basic elements of the art form in which I am creating and I use them in my composition. • I study the work of great artists to get ideas for improving my own compositions.	• I use the appropriate instruments or tools. • I can control the tools and/or media I am using. • I am careful when I work and pay attention to details. • I practice using the concepts, skills, and tools I am learning.	• I think of ways to show imagination in my composition. • I build new and interesting ideas into my composition.	• I create a draft of my composition. • I learn specific skills that I need to complete each composition. • I revise my composition and produce a final product.		• If my creation is a performing arts composition, I perform it or have others perform it. • If my creation is a visual arts composition, I display it. • I evaluate my work with others and get ideas about how I can improve.
Score:	Score:	Score:	Score:		Score:
Comments:					

6	Exemplary Work: My work is exceptional and demonstrates that I use this trait at a very sophisticated level.
5	Accomplished Work: My work demonstrates that I am fluent in using this trait.
4	Progressing Work: My work demonstrates that my use of this trait is adequate and that I am improving all the time.
3	Developing Work: My work is in transition from weak use of this trait to adequate use of this trait.
2	Beginning Work: My work shows that I am a novice - I am beginning to develop this trait.
1	Not Present: My work shows that I have not yet developed this trait or this trait is not present in this performance.

Figure 6.4 Artistic composition scoring guide

"But what do these projects and performances tell me about my teaching?," you may be asking. Step out of this sea of "stuff," and climb the hill of perception[3] to look for common clues about your teaching. Did some part of a project appear to be weak in most student work? Does the class share some common misconceptions that can be addressed in a future lesson? Are there instructions provided for this work that can be tightened up to produce better performances? What common pitfalls did most students fall into that can be shaped in future

Name:		Date:		
Uses the Writing Process	Ideas/Content	Organization	Style	Conventions
I prewrite, create a first draft, edit and revise my writing and publish a final draft.	My writing is clear and my ideas are well developed.	The sequence of my writing has order and makes sense.	Words, Sentences, Voice I write words and sentences that are varied and interesting and that make the reader feel as if they are talking to a real person.	I show that I know and can use standard writing conventions.
• Before I start writing, I create many ideas about which to write. • I think about what I already know about the topic. • I create a first draft in which I concentrate on getting all of my ideas down. • I carefully revise my draft to improve the words, sentences, organization, spelling and punctuation.	• I clearly express ideas in my writing. • I develop these ideas with supporting details. • I select an appropriate form in which to express my ideas. • I write in such a way that readers will stay interested. • I edit my writing to improve my ideas.	• I have a beginning introduction, a middle, and an ending conclusion in my writing. • I develop my ideas in some order. • When I edit my writing, I identify ways to improve the organization.	• I bring a topic to life. • I write in a way that sounds natural and that matches the language my characters would actually use. • I choose to use clear and interesting words that match my purpose. • I use words that create strong imagery. • I use a mixture of simple and complex sentences in my writing.	• I use correct punctuation and capital letters in my writing. • I use correct grammar in my writing. • I use correct spelling in my writing. • I edit my writing or have someone edit my writing to correct for these conventions.
Score:	Score:	Score:	Score:	Score:

Comments:

6	Exemplary Work: My work is exceptional and demonstrates that I use this trait at a very sophisticated level.
5	Accomplished Work: My work demonstrates that I am fluent in using this trait.
4	Progressing Work: My work demonstrates that my use of this trait is adequate and that I am improving all the time.
3	Developing Work: My work is in transition from weak use of this trait to adequate use of this trait.
2	Beginning Work: My work shows that I am a novice - I am beginning to develop this trait.
1	Not Present: My work shows that I have not yet developed this trait or this trait is not present in this performance.

Figure 6.5 Writing Scoring Guide

lessons? Are there ways that I can make each student more autonomous and self-directed in the learning process?

We have more and better tools to use in teaching and evaluating student products—both their use of key processes (procedural knowledge) and their acquisition of key facts and concepts from subject disciplines (declarative knowledge). Where we find much difficulty is in getting students to reveal their metacognition; that is, the thinking behind their work. This metacognition is critical in the learning process. It is critical to get students to think aloud about their thinking.

To tap students' conditional knowledge—their metacognitive awareness—as well as reinforce the use of key strategies (see Figure 2.2 in chapter 2), we have developed a set of bookmarks that prompt students to apply specific strategies at specific stages in their work. This forces them to think about the why, how, and when of their strategy use (see Figure 6.6).

For example, when students are assigned a substantive project and they need assistance in tracking what to do next and next, have them pull out the bookmark on "planning." They can read the prompts and use them to determine a work plan. Or, you can hand them the "information gathering" bookmark to assist them in identifying how they will get the needed information for the project.

Prepare Strategies

Prepare Surveying:	What do I already know about this? What do I have to work with here? What do I need before I can start? What is the situation now? What has been done to get to this point?

Prepare Retrieving:	What do I already know that I could use here? Do I remember anything about this topic? What comes to mind when I think of _____? How would I describe this? Can I think of anything that might help me with this project?

Prepare Planning:	What is my timeline to complete this project? What do I need to do first? Next? Last? What are the parts of this project and when do they need to be completed? What should I get started on first? Will I need help with anything and who will I get to help me?

Prepare Forecasting:	Do I have any questions before I start? What is the central question here? What questions might I want to ask before I start? What questions do I need to be able to answer at the end of this project? What might happen next? What might cause this?

First Dare Strategies

First Dare Focusing:	What is important to pay attention to here? What is the problem here? What are my goals? What are the two or three most important points to consider? In one or two sentences what does this tell me?

First Dare Information Gathering:	What information do I have? What information do I need? What else do I need to complete this project? Where will I get what I need? Am I keeping track of where I am getting the information I need?

First Dare Self regulating:	What am I thinking now? Where am I with this project now? How are things coming together here? What's going on in my head right now? At what step am I in the process?

Figure 6.6 Metacognitive question prompts

First Dare Generating:	Can I think of anything else to do here? What am I learning that's new? Have I come up with any new ideas/insights? What are the possibilities? What are the alternatives?
First Dare Organizing:	In what way might I track this information as I get it? What is the gist of this so far? Do I have a system for keeping track of all of this? Is the system I'm using to track information working for me? Could I use a chart, a concept map, outline to organize this information?

Repair Strategies

Repair Fixing-up:	Is there anything puzzling to me? Does this make sense to me? Do these ideas work together? Am I comfortable with my thinking right now? Where am I experiencing difficulty?
Repair Evaluating:	Are these ideas of any value? Does this information seem reliable to me? What seems to work or not work here? How do I know that this work is any good? Why is _____ significant?
Repair Analyzing:	What are the different parts of _____? What are the essential features of this model/concept/idea? What are the critical attributes of _____? What evidence do I have to think this? What is the relationship between _____ and _____?
Repair Perspective-taking:	What might others say about this? Who might be interested in this and how might they respond? What other points of view might there be about this? How might _____ view this? Who are the stakeholders here and what are their positions?

Share Strategies

Share Integrating:	How do these parts fit together? In what ways can I connect all of this together? What ideas can I add to this? How can I put this together in a meaningful way? What might happen if I combined _____ and _____?

Figure 6.6 Metacognitive question prompts (*continued*)

Share Organizing:	How can I organize this information in a way that makes sense to others? Which ideas are most important here? Can I cluster ideas here around two or three big concepts? How can I describe this concept so that others can understand? How will I decide which parts of the project to share?

Share Presenting:	In what ways might I share what I have learned? Who is my audience and how might I best share with them? How can I share this information with accuracy? In what way can I get my main points across to my audience? Do I want to share this information in more than one format? If so what?

Figure 6.6 Metacognitive question prompts (*continued*)

One more thing you can do to get feedback about your teaching is to simply ask students how things are going for them.

Rule #6: Simply Ask

You can ask for feedback orally in class; however, we find that students won't be as candid in class as they might be if they can anonymously provide feedback. I (Betty) invite students to give written feedback and "lay it on me" at the door as they leave class. I make it clear that their perceptions of class experiences are critical to share with me and that there will be no consequences for those sharing negative feedback. Figure 6.7 shows the form I use.

Tell me how you feel about class today. Put a check in the box. From your point of view:

1. Did the lesson go too slow or too fast today?	Too Slow	About Right	Too Fast
2. How would you rate the help I gave you today?	No help and/or Not helpful	Help About Right	Too helpful
3. Did the lesson make sense for you?	Made no sense	Made some sense	Make a lot of sense
4. Was there enough activity in class today?	Too little activity	Activity just right	Too much activity
5. Did you feel safe to express yourself in class?	Not safe	O.K.	Very safe
Class would be better if . . .			

Figure 6.7 "Lay It On Me" Feedback Form

The form is written to use with older students, although I have used it with younger students as well. I make an overhead of the form and project it in class. As I go over the text on the overhead, younger students follow along and mark their own forms.

I want to make one more point here. As I stand at the classroom door, I keep one hand out to collect the forms. With my other hand, I give 'em five and thank each for the feedback as they leave. I don't ever look at the feedback in the presence of students. In the morning (or during the next class), I usually summarize the data and pledge to work together with the class to improve. It is a team effort, and modeling my willingness to get honest feedback allows me to give honest feedback. Keep these feedback forms together with other evidence of the ACES in your pedagogiofolio.

Another simple adaptation of this for younger students involves bringing a stuffed animal with their own mailbox into the classroom. When teaching first through third graders, I had a stuffed cat with big diamond rhinestone eyes named Cleo (see chapter 5). Cleo sat on the shelf by its mailbox surveying the classroom. Students were asked to write a simple note to Cleo to express any concerns or joys about the workings of the class. Cleo would then write a note back to each student who wrote to her. At times, I would get concerns expressed about instructional issues and at times get concerns about friendships and group dynamics. This was good, as all of these factors contribute to student growth.

End your evaluation by conducting simple action research in your classroom. We highly recommend the work of Richard Sagor. In his book, *How to Conduct Collaborative Action Research*,[4] Sagor describes how teachers can use a collaborative action research process to improve the teaching-learning process and make meaningful contributions to the development of the teaching profession. He defines action research as a disciplined process of inquiry conducted by and for those taking the action. The primary reason for engaging in action research is to assist the "actor" in improving and/or refining his or her actions.[5] Sagor states that,

> Educational action research can be engaged in by a single teacher, by a group of colleagues who share an interest in a common problem, or by the entire faculty of a school. Whatever the scenario, action research always involves the same seven-step process. These seven steps, which become an endless cycle for the inquiring teacher, are the following:
>
> 1. Selecting a focus
> 2. Clarifying theories
> 3. Identifying research questions
> 4. Collecting data
> 5. Analyzing data
> 6. Reporting results
> 7. Taking informed action[6]

This book is loaded with new tools for you to use in your classroom. Several tools are provided to help students prepare, first dare, and so forth. Using Sagor's model, try using similar tools with different classes or different units to compare the results that you get. Some tools for retrieving may work better with your class(es) than another retrieving tool. The same is true for repairing tools and sharing tools. Try them out and see which seem to work better in your setting.

In Summary: Be a Data Nut

We have shared many ideas here for evaluating the effectiveness of your instruction. We suggested that you PAY ATTENTION ALL THE WAY by: (a) planning instruction carefully to incorporate best practices, (b) keeping a record of your instruction in a pedagogiofolio, (c) by using ACES to pick up clues—cognitive, behavioral, and intuitive clues from students, (d) by conducting simple action research in your classes, and (e) by asking students explicitly to give you feedback. This all adds up to a membership in the "Data Nut Club." We actually have a group of educators in our district who call themselves the "Data Nuts." They get together about once every six weeks. Each brings their own pedagogiofolio and shares. Others discuss the data, give feedback, and make suggestions for improvement. Let's look at some examples.

In our school district, we administer a reading diagnostic test to all K–5 students in the fall and in the spring. The results of the assessments are stored in the district's database and posted on the Web in a secure location accessible only to those staff authorized to view the data. Figure 6.8 shows the scores for a class of third graders in the fall of 2001.

District norms were established for the 2001–2002 year. They are listed in Figure 6.9.

Student Name	Grade	High Frequency Words 2^2	3^1	3^2	Reading Rate RR	Listening Comprehension MC	OE	Reading Comprehension MC	OE
Bill	03		24	22	49			5	1
Christina	03		24	24	155			5	2
Betsy	03	14	14		20	4	1		
Kyle	03	21	18	15	41			4	4
Maria	03		21	24	73			5	2
Cody	03		24	24	134			3	2
Darlene	03		24	24	94			5	4
Penny	03		20	19	86			4	4
McKenzie	03		20	23	96			5	3
John	03	9	12		28	2	1		
Al	03		22	22	75			5	4
Patrick	03		24	24	134			4	4
Lisa	03		23	22	44			4	4
Nancy	03		20	15	31	4	1		
Robyn	03		24	24	129			4	3
Ian	03		24	24	68			4	4
Jessica	03		19	16	33	2	1		
Karen	03		24	24	154			5	4
Felicia	03		24	24	129			2	1
José	03		24	23	131			5	4
Hailey	03		24	22	124			5	4
Taylor	03	16	8		18	5	4		
Taryn	03		21	23	99			5	4
Teresa	03		24	24	114			4	4
Tim	03		23	20	72			2	1

1. The testing protocol called for the student to read the 3^1 high frequency word list first. Each list consists of 24 words. If the student scored 18 or less correct, the tester then gave him the 2^2 list to read. If the student read 19 words or more, he was given the 3^2 list to read.
2. Students whose reading rate (RR) was 40 words a minute or less were read the story and questions for comprehension purposes. These scores are listed here as Listening Comprehension. Students reading 41 words a minute correctly were instructed to read the comprehension passage out loud to the tester and answer the questions aloud.
3. The comprehension questions consisted of 5 multiple choice (MC) questions and 2 open-ended (OE) questions.

Figure 6.8 Scores on reading diagnostic test, Fall 2001

The charts below provide you with norms for each of the reading assessments in the Diagnostic Reading Kits. Use this data to interpret your students' results. Remember, you can retrieve the scores for your whole class on the web. See the attached directions to access the data.

In some cases, the raw scores were so similar (the range of responses were so similar) that when we broke them out into the quartiles, the scores in the chart are the same or nearly the same. This was true for the comprehension questions and the high frequency word lists.

Third Grade

Subtest: High Frequency Words – 3^1 (Total possible = 24 in 40 seconds)	Fall	Spring
10%ile	19	23
25%ile	19	24
50%ile	23	24
75%ile	24	24
90%ile	24	24

Third Grade

Subtest: High Frequency Words – 3^2 (Total possible = 24 in 40 seconds)	Fall	Spring
10%ile	20	22
25%ile	23	24
50%ile	24	24
75%ile	24	24
90%ile	24	24

Third Grade

Subtest: Oral Reading Rate – Correct Words Per Minute	Fall	Spring
10%ile	27	47
25%ile	55	78
50%ile	81	107
75%ile	111	149
90%ile	139	168

Third Grade

Subtest: Comprehension Multiple Choice (Total Possible = 5)	Fall	Spring
10%ile	3	4
25%ile	4	5
50%ile	5	5
75%ile	5	5
90%ile	5	5

Third Grade

Subtest: Comprehension Open-ended (Total possible = 4)	Fall	Spring
10%ile	1	2
25%ile	2	3
50%ile	3	4
75%ile	4	4
90%ile	4	4

Figure 6.9 Third-grade reading norms 2001–2002

Using the data in Figure 6.8 and the norms in Figure 6.9, the "data nuts" determined those students needing specific intervention, as well as those students whose test scores indicated a need for swift intervention by the school's student support team working in conjunction with the school psychologist and the parents. Figure 6.10 shows the results of their analysis of the data. Those rows shaded in gray represent students who have priority for further testing and referral for special services in the district.

Interestingly, one of the data nuts thought it would be interesting to compare the results of the district's reading assessment with two other assessments that she had used in the past. As a special education teacher, she decided to give her

	Refer to SST Team	Need Phonics Intervention	Need High Frequency Intervention	Need Fluency Intervention	Need Comprehension Strategies
Bill	√	√		√	
Betsy	√	√	√	√	√
Kyle	√	√	√	√	
Maria				√	
Cody					√ recheck
Penny			√	√	
John	√	√	√	√	√
Al			√	√	
Lisa	√	√	√	√	
Nancy	√	√	√	√	√
Ian				√	
Jessica	√	√	√	√	√
Felicia					√
Taylor	√	√	√	√	
Tim			√	√	√

The SST Team (the Student Support Team) in Eugene School District reviews referrals for further testing by the school psychologist.

Figure 6.10 The data nuts analysis of third-grade testing data

learning center students an oral reading fluency passage that was developed in another district by special educators. She also gave an oral reading fluency passage developed at a nearby university. She found that each passage produced dramatically different results. Figure 6.11 shows the results for one of her students.

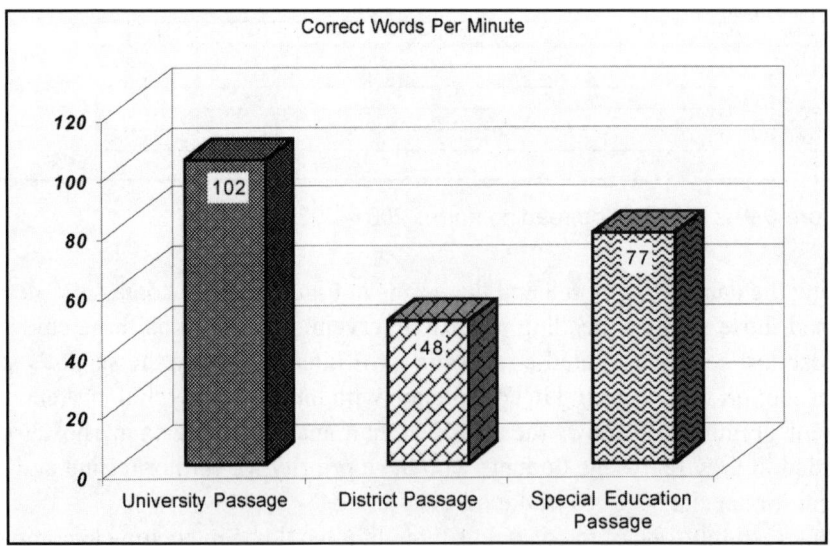

Figure 6.11 A comparison of one student's reading rate using three different measures

This has led district-level administrators to take a closer look at the validity of the passages being recommended for use in different settings in the district.

It is important to note that one rule in the Data Nut group is "No whining." The focus is on "can do" and "what if." What evidence do I have that what I am doing actually contributes to student growth and achievement? What can I do to improve my odds? What if I try it this way instead of that way? Together, they are having a smashing good time planting the seeds of growth in their own pedagogy!

End Notes

1. For further information on the work of these researchers, we encourage you to visit the Web sites of both schools of education. They can be found at <http://www.lrdc.pitt.edu/> and at <http://www.gse.harvard.edu/>.

2. Lewin, L. & Shoemaker, B. (1998). Great performances: Creating classroom-based assessment tasks. Alexandria, Virginia: Association for Supervision and Curriculum Development, p. 112.

3. We adapted this phrase from Barry Lane in his excellent book, *After the end: Teaching and learning creative revision.* Portsmouth, New Hampshire: Heinemann.

4. Sagor, R. (1992). How to conduct collaborative action research. Alexandria, VA: Association for Supervision and Curriculum Development.

5. This definition is from workshop materials from the Institute for the Study of Inquiry in Education (ISIE), 602 NE 3rd Ave., Suite E-174, Camas, WA 98607. Phone: 360-834-3503. E-mail: rdsagor@isie.org (n.d.).

6. Sagor, R. (1992). Ibid.

CHAPTER SEVEN

Teacher-to-Teacher

"She's Teaching With a Full Deck"

She has been trained in and uses a full complement of teaching tools.

Our goal has been to equip you, the reader, with a large repertoire of methods to use in helping students more effectively construct meaning around content knowledge from various disciplines. We have attempted to facilitate teacher-to-teacher exchange of practical, hands-on tools that can be easily adapted to each reader's own specific teaching setting.

As we stated in the Introduction, "Just as a card player cannot be successful when missing a number of cards, teachers cannot be successful in increasing achievement of all students when they are limited in the number of methods with which they can teach."

So to wrap it up, let's explore several notions we have attempted to develop in this book by using a number of card game expressions. Our friend and colleague, Kay Mehas, interviewed us to summarize our work here.

> **Kay:** If you could describe in one or two sentences the thesis of this book, what would it be?

Larry: Teachers can guarantee that they will have a "hot" instructional hand when they expand the number of cards in their teaching deck. So the thesis here is to increase your repertoire of instructional methods and strengthen your pedagogy (be smart enough to know when to use which strategy) and student achievement will increase.

Betty: Yes, when teachers play with a full deck, they not only close the achievement gap, they equip more students to clear the bar of high academic standards.

Kay: A gambler, as Kenny Rogers sang, has to know when to hold them and know when to fold them, know when to walk away, and know when to run. What does this have to do with teaching? Are you saying that teachers are gamblers?

Betty: Well, in this case, we are using the card metaphor to reinforce the notion that good teaching occurs when teachers have many instructional tools to draw from and are smart enough to know when to use them; that is, know when to hold them, know when to fold them. However, teachers do gamble, in a way. They use their best professional judgment to assess student needs and then gamble that the strategies they use with that student or group of students will be successful. And like gamblers, teachers are observant, in that they attend to what cards have been played, noting the effects of the use of different tools on student growth; and they attend to the other players, the students, picking up cues as to how things are going.

Kay: You've heard the expression, "playing your cards close to your vest." What implication does this idiom have for teachers? Should teachers play their cards close to their vests?

Betty: First, I want to say that I am glad we were dealt this hand; that is, that Christopher-Gordon Publishers gave us this opportunity to write on this subject. But I need you to know that our hand would not be nearly as strong had we kept our cards close to our vests. When we took the risk to open our classrooms and to share methodology with each other, our teaching improved.

Larry: Yes, I agree. Teachers should lay their cards on the table—both for their colleagues to see and for their students to see. Let's explore that more.

It has been said that teaching, in many ways, is the loneliest profession. With the increased class sizes and workloads that many school districts are experiencing, teachers—just to stay afloat—often are forced to stay in their classrooms, rarely having time to visit with each other. It's tragic, because we know that teachers are like students. They can and do learn from each other. Hopefully, this book will serve as a vehicle for teachers to share more with each other.

Betty: Yes, yes, yes! We have included here a number of tools that others have developed. We want teachers who read this book, and who have ideas or examples to share, to definitely get in touch with us. That is the way we all learn.

Larry: And it is important for teachers to lay their cards on the table for students. As we described in chapter 4, teachers need to model for students. This modeling is then followed by guided practice, where students shape their performances based on the modeling of teachers.

Kay: One card idiom I remember from my childhood is "Read 'em and weep." What does that mean and does it have anything to do with teaching?

Betty: When I was younger, I thought "read 'em and weep" meant that my hand was so much stronger than yours. I thought that if I used this expression, I was announcing to others at the table that if they could see my hand, they would weep. Using that interpretation, I would say, "Expand your teaching methods and others will be so impressed that they will "read 'em and weep."

Larry: Betty now understands that the expression means expressing dissatisfaction with one's own hand. So now we say, "If you are constantly frustrated with the tools you have to work with or if you know intuitively that the methods you are using are not working with some or all of your students, then don't sit around weeping. Expand your teaching deck with more and better tools. Then when the cards are dealt, you can read 'em and shout!"

Kay: Any parting words of advice to educators?

Betty and Larry: "Yes! Isn't it great to be teaching with a full deck!"

Appendix

Brainy Light Bulb

Name _____ Date _____

Appendix 147

Mental Floppy Disk

Name _____   Date _____

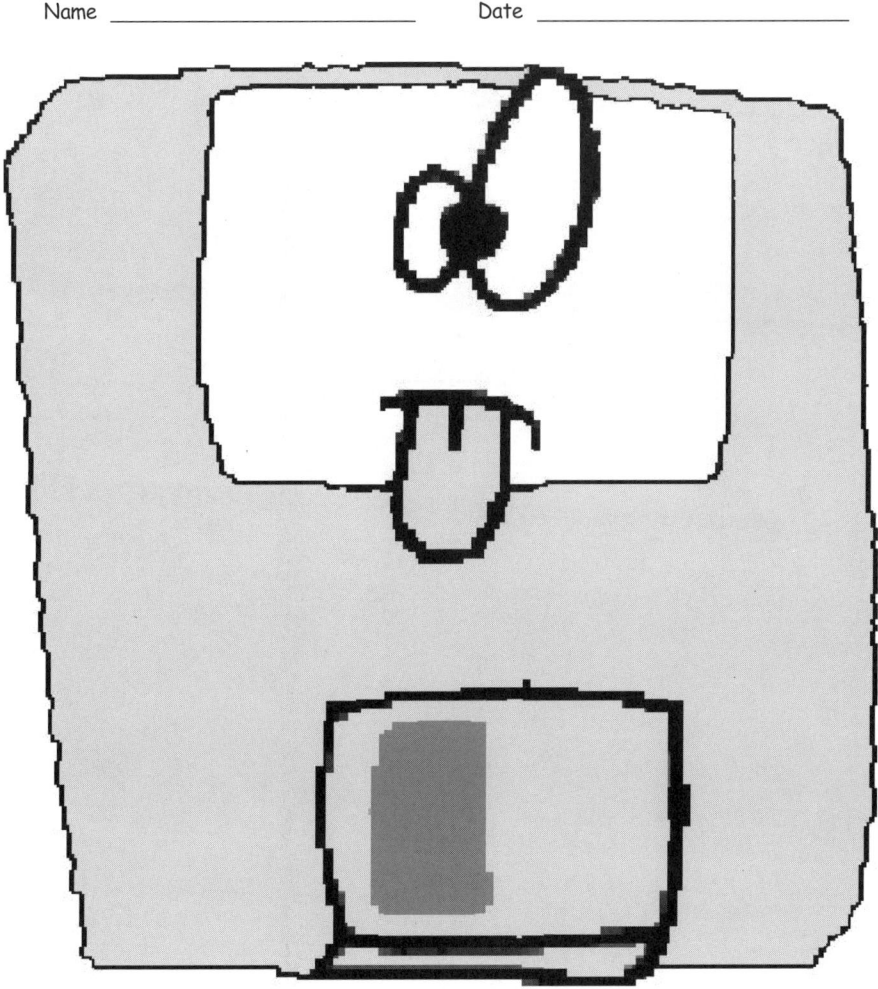

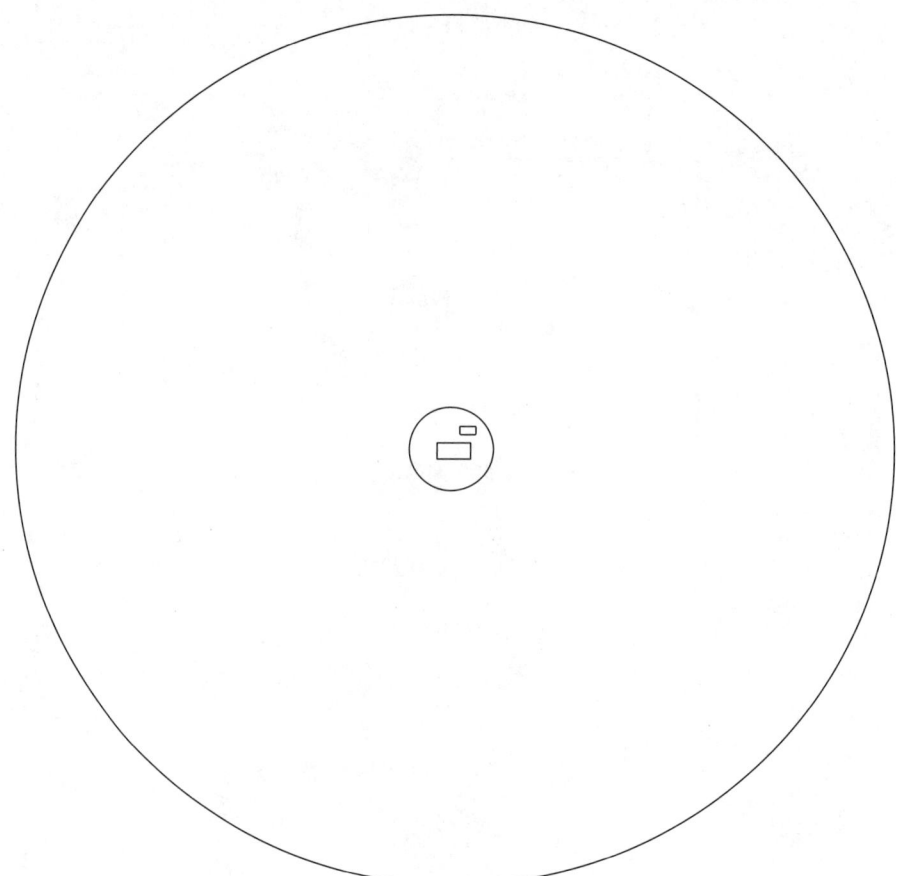

Name _____   Date _____

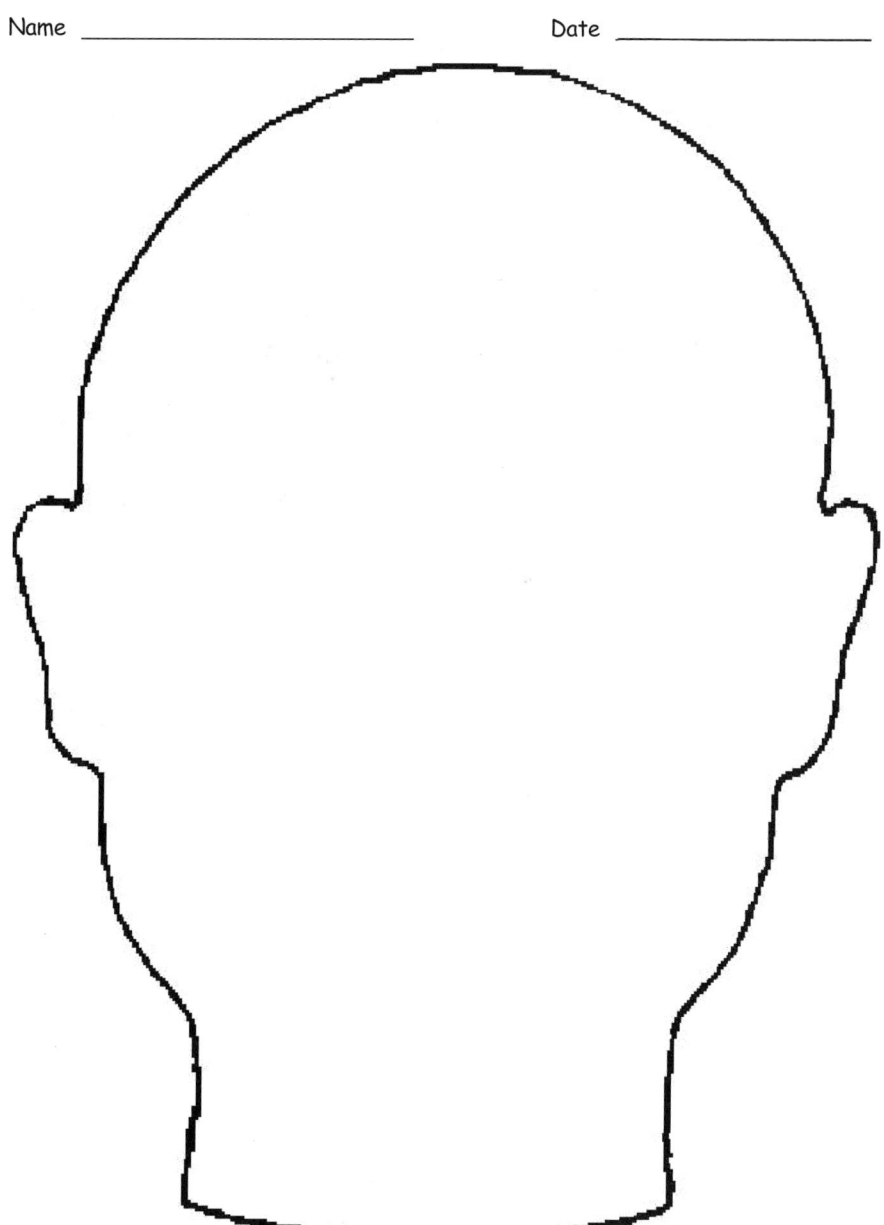

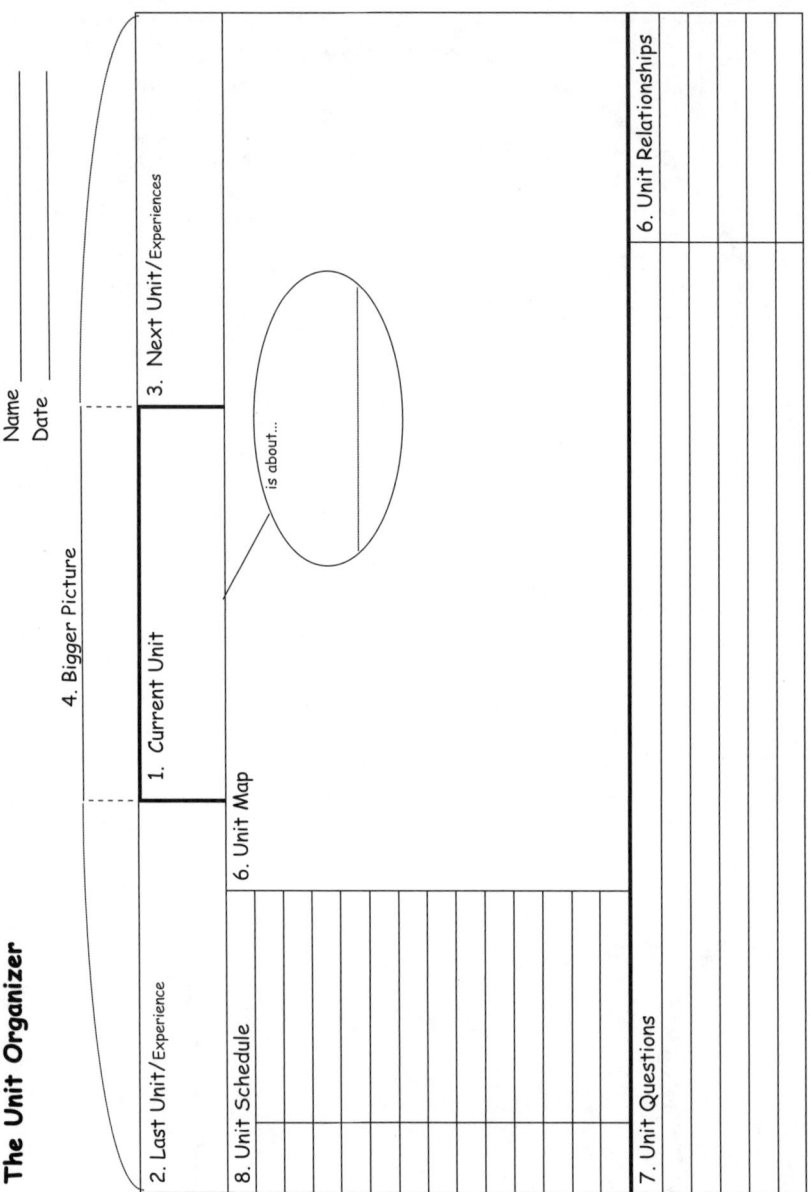

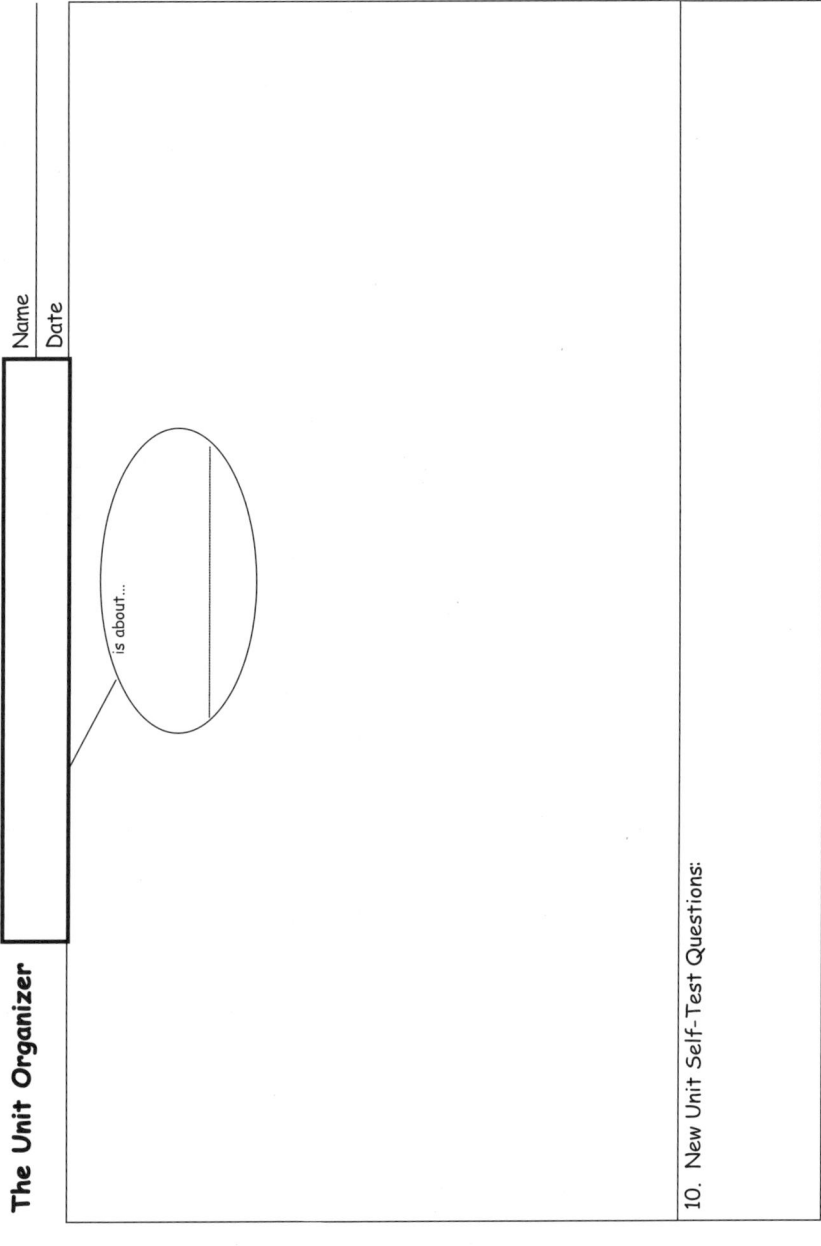

Name _____   Date _____

Date	Time	Goal	Materials	Completed	
				Yes	No

Work Plan For _____   Date _____

Date	Time	Goal	Materials	Yes!	No

Photo Album

Name _____ Date _____ Act/Scene: _____

Appendix

Name _____ Date _____

The Adapted Value Examination Matrix

1. Identify the rule, concept, or issue to be analyzed. Record it in the top box numbered 1.
2. Take a position either for or against the statement, concept, or issue. Write that position in boxes 2 or 3.
3. Then record your reasoning or logic behind your position in 2a or 3a. After completing your position, take the opposite or an alternative position and analyze it.

1. Record the statement, concept or issue here:	
2. Assigned Value **For**:	3. Assigned Value **Against**:
2a. Reasoning or Logic Behind My Value:	3a. Reasoning or Logic Behind My Value:

I-Search Chart

Name _____ Date _____ Teacher _____

Initial When Done	Step	Things to Do
	Step 1:	**Prepare:** What is the topic you will be researching? Write the topic at the top of the next page, and on this line. _____
	Step 2:	**Prepare:** On the lines provided, list 8-10 questions about this topic that you would like to answer. Write only one question per line.
	Step 3:	**First Dare:** Find the answers to these questions using reference books, encyclopedias, and/or magazines. When you find an answer, JOT words and phrases that answer the question in the space under each question. DO NOT COPY sentences directly from the reference book. Write on only ONE SIDE OF THE PAPER.
	Step 4:	**First Dare:** Create a list of sources you used by copying the name of the book/magazine/encyclopedia and the page number(s) used on the <u>reference list worksheet</u>. This will be attached to your report at the end and will be called "Works Cited."
	Step 5:	**First Dare:** After you have found the answers to all of your questions, cut the sections apart so that each of your original questions is on a separate smaller piece of paper.
	Step 6:	**First Dare:** Place all of your questions on a table and cluster the questions together that seem to belong together. When you are sure that you have the sections in the best order, tape them back together on sheets of blank paper and write a name for that cluster at the top of each cluster. You now have a VERY ROUGH DRAFT.
	Step 7:	**Repair:** Rewrite the VERY ROUGH DRAFT into a ROUGH DRAFT by making all of your notes into complete sentences. Each individual section of paper will become one paragraph. Rewrite your sentences as necessary to make them flow one to another and to make them interesting. Plan to have at least 3 sentences in each paragraph.
	Step 8:	**Repair:** Work together with an adult in class to edit your ROUGH DRAFT. Check your spelling and your punctuation as well as be sure to have no sentences that go on and on and on. Mark changes you want to make on this rough draft with a different colored pencil so that you can see the changes easily.
	Step 9:	**Share:** Using suggestions and advice provided by the adult who helped you edit, rewrite the report as a FINAL DRAFT. Write carefully so that your copy will be as near perfect as you can make it.
	Step 10:	**Share:** Work together with an adult to take the information off of the reference list worksheet and create a "Works Cited" page.
	Step 11:	**Share:** Attach your completed "Works Cited List" to the back of your report. Place your completed report and works cited list in a manila folder along with your very rough draft and your rough draft.
	Step 12:	**Share:** Pat yourself on the back for completing your very first research report.

Appendix 157

My Topic _____

My Questions:

1. _____
   _____?

2. _____
   _____?

3. _____
   _____?

4. _____
   _____?

5. _____
   _____?

6. _____
   _____?

7. _____
   _____?

8. _____
   _____?

9. _____
   _____?

10. _____

_____?

11. _____

_____?

12. _____

_____?

Appendix

Reference List Worksheet

First Source:

Circle One: Book   Newspaper   Magazine   Encyclopedia   Interview   Website
Author/s Names:
Publication Date: Title:
Location of Publisher (City and State):
Publisher Name: Page Numbers:
Website Address (URL):

Second Source:

Circle One: Book   Newspaper   Magazine   Encyclopedia   Interview   Website
Author/s Names:
Publication Date: Title:
Location of Publisher (City and State):
Publisher Name: Page Numbers:
Website Address (URL):

Third Source:

Circle One: Book   Newspaper   Magazine   Encyclopedia   Interview   Website
Author/s Names:
Publication Date: Title:
Location of Publisher (City and State):
Publisher Name: Page Numbers:
Website Address (URL):

Fourth Source:

Circle One: Book   Newspaper   Magazine   Encyclopedia   Interview   Website
Author/s Names:
Publication Date: Title:
Location of Publisher (City and State):
Publisher Name: Page Numbers:
Website Address (URL):

Reference List Worksheet continued

Fifth Source:

Circle One: Book Newspaper Magazine Encyclopedia Interview Website	
Author/s Names:	
Publication Date:	Title:
Location of Publisher (City and State):	
Publisher Name:	Page Numbers:
Website Address (URL):	

Sixth Source:

Circle One: Book Newspaper Magazine Encyclopedia Interview Website	
Author/s Names:	
Publication Date:	Title:
Location of Publisher (City and State):	
Publisher Name:	Page Numbers:
Website Address (URL):	

Seventh Source:

Circle One: Book Newspaper Magazine Encyclopedia Interview Website	
Author/s Names:	
Publication Date:	Title:
Location of Publisher (City and State):	
Publisher Name:	Page Numbers:
Website Address (URL):	

Eighth Source:

Circle One: Book Newspaper Magazine Encyclopedia Interview Website	
Author/s Names:	
Publication Date:	Title:
Location of Publisher (City and State):	
Publisher Name:	Page Numbers:
Website Address (URL):	

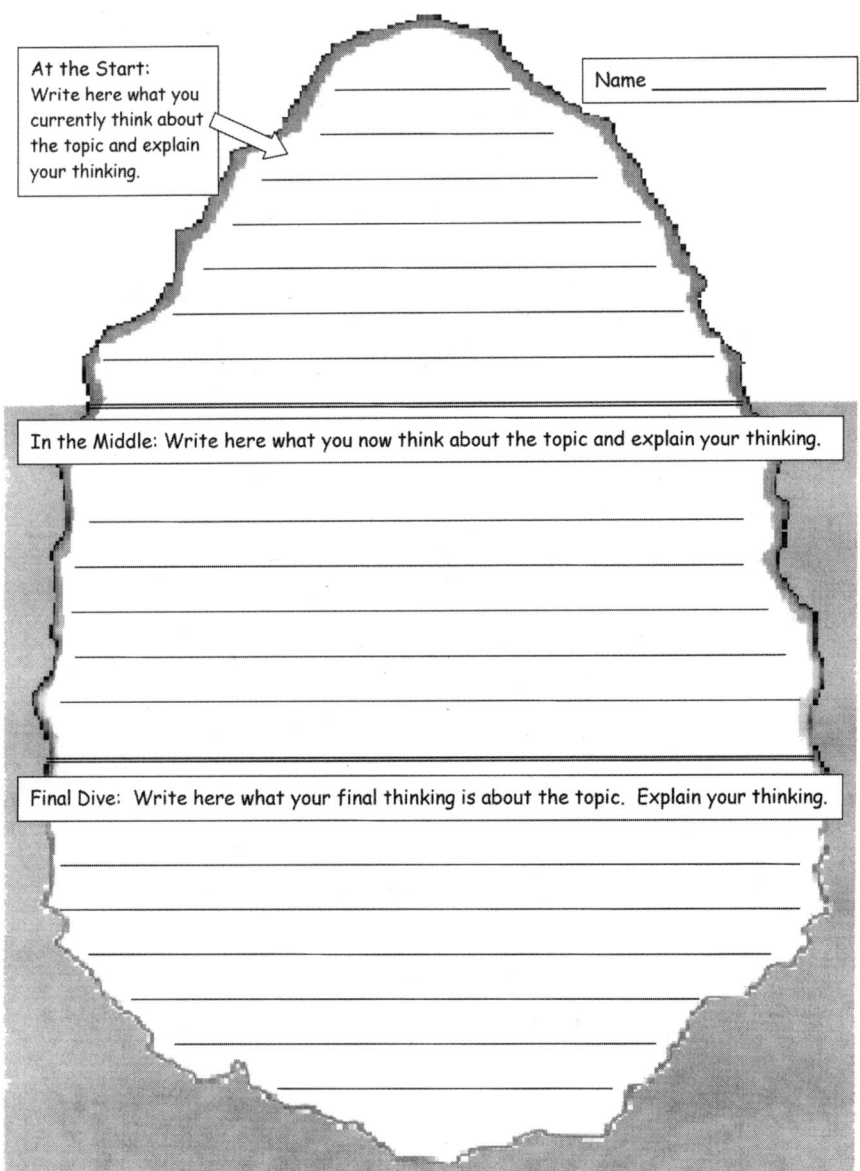

Name _____   Date _____

Record the vocabulary word in the center box. Record your responses the prompts in the outer boxes.

Appendix

User Friendly Text Checklist

More and more educators are acknowledging that many textbooks are written and formatted in such a way that make it difficult for students – particularly lower-performing students – to construct meaning around the content included in the text. Some texts are simply more "considerate" to the learner than others. To help teachers identify which texts might be a better match for students we have identified a number of traits that are present in user friendly text – "**U F T**" for short. Use the following checklist to evaluate the printed materials you use with your students.

Text _____   Pages Analyzed _____

Use the following scale:
1   This trait is not present in the text.
2   This trait is present but weak in the text.
3   This trait is present and adequate in the text.
4   This trait is present and strong in the text.

Vocabulary: The text...	1	2	3	4
1. Sets off important vocabulary words critical to understanding the text in boldface or color print?				
2. Provides a pronunciation key for important vocabulary words?				
3. Explicitly teaches the word and the concept it refers to **in** the text?				
4. Provides an easy-to-use glossary?				

Text Structure and Concept Development The text...	1	2	3	4
1. Includes a table of contents or outline of key points?				
2. Includes an introduction to the topic stating key chapter or unit concepts clearly?				
3. Includes a summary of key points at the end of the section, chapter, or unit?				
4. As appropriate, includes headings and subheadings to cue the reader as to the main ideas and structure of the passage?				
5. Includes subheadings that relate directly to the main headings?				
6. Uses colors, shapes, font styles, and placement of headings to distinguish between main and subheadings?				
7. Includes a title that reflects the main idea of the chapter or section?				
8. Includes key questions that focus on a balance of factual details, major concepts and critical thinking?				

Graphics: The text...	1	2	3	4
1. Includes illustrations, charts, and graphs that enhance the most important information in the text?				
2. Includes illustrations, charts, and graphs that break up the text to make it more accessible to struggling readers?				
3. Includes charts and graphs that share key information in a clear and concise format?				
4. Includes easy to read legends to interpret data in charts and graphs?				

Appendix 167

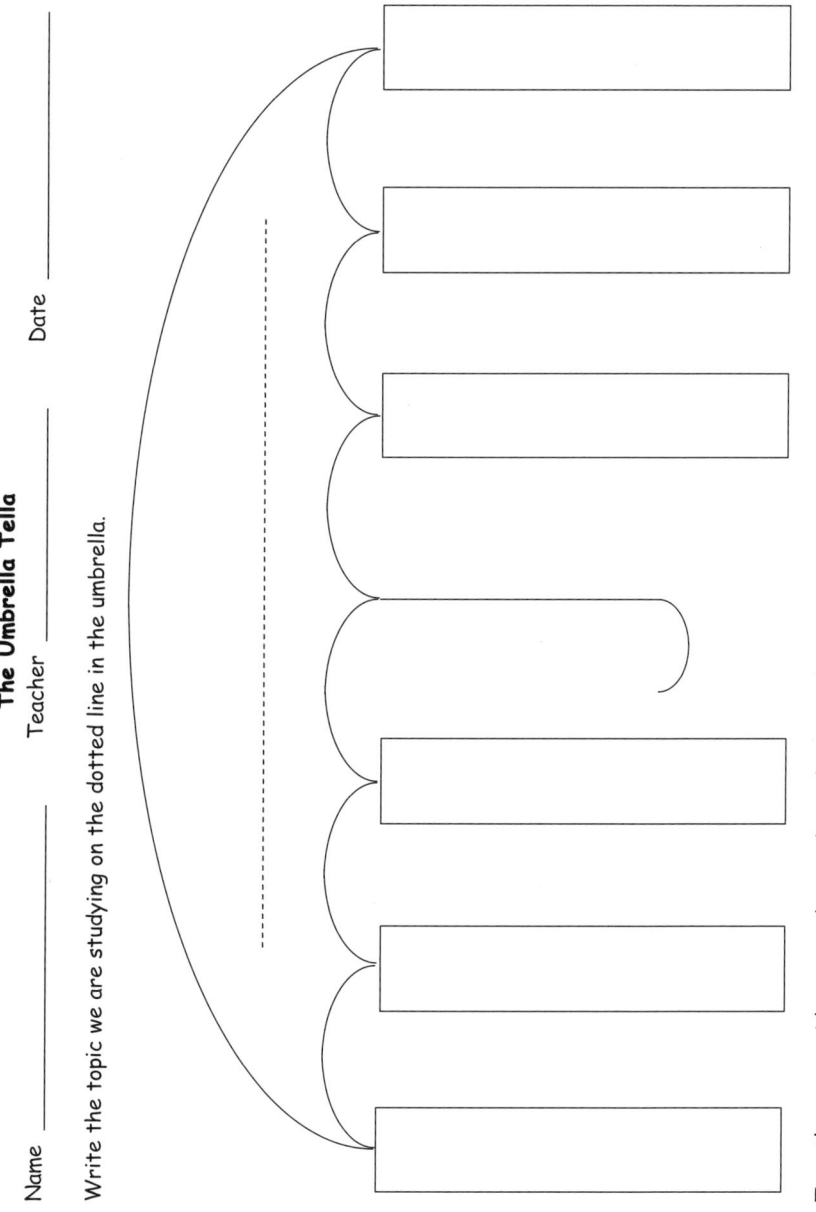

Date ____

Name ____

Appendix 169

Date

Name

"Lay It On Me" Feedback Form

Tell me how you feel about class today. Put a check in the box. From your point of view:

1. Did the lesson go too slow or too fast today?	Too Slow	About Right	Too Fast
2. How would you rate the help I gave you today?	No help and/or Not helpful	Help About Right	Too helpful
3. Did the lesson make sense for you?	Made no sense	Made some sense	Make a lot of sense
4. Was there enough activity in class today?	Too little activity	Activity just right	Too much activity
5. Did you feel safe to express yourself in class?	Not safe	O.K.	

Class would be better if.....

"Lay It On Me" Feedback Form

Tell me how you feel about class today. Put a check in the box. From your point of view:

1. Did the lesson go too slow or too fast today?	Too Slow	About Right	Too Fast
2. How would you rate the help I gave you today?	No help and/or Not helpful	Help About Right	Too helpful
3. Did the lesson make sense for you?	Made no sense	Made some sense	Make a lot of sense
4. Was there enough activity in class today?	Too little activity	Activity just right	Too much activity
5. Did you feel safe to express yourself in class?	Not safe	O.K.	

Class would be better if.....

About the Authors

Dr. Betty Jean Eklund Shoemaker

Dr. Betty Jean Shoemaker is a curriculum and staff development coordinator for Eugene Public School District 4J in Eugene, Oregon. She has taught in both regular and special education classrooms since 1965.

In her current position, she works districtwide to provide instructional leadership and to develop curriculum and assessment resources for staff. In addition, she provides professional development to administrators, teachers, and instructional assistants.

Betty earned her PhD at the University of Oregon in Curriculum and Instruction. She consults nationally in the areas of integrated thematic curriculum, performance-based assessment, and teaching methodology. She has published work in *Education Leadership, Phi Delta Kappan,* and *Reoper Review*. In addition, she and coauthor, Larry Lewin, have written a book on performance assessment titled, *Great Performances: Creating Classroom-Based Assessment Tasks.*

Larry Lewin

Larry Lewin, a classroom teacher for 24 years at the elementary, middle, and high school levels in Oregon, now consults nationally on educational topics of interest, including Integrating the Internet into Instruction, Classroom-Based Performance Assessment, Practical Strategies for Helping Struggling Readers and Writers, and Teaching with a Full Deck: Innovative Instructional Strategies.

In addition to presenting for school districts in 46 U.S. states, five Canadian provinces, and two states in Mexico, Larry has appeared at numerous national- and state-level professional conferences.

Larry is the author of *Using the Internet to Strengthen Curriculum* (ASCD, May, 2001), the coauthor with Betty Shoemaker of *Great Performances: Creating Classroom-Based Assessment Tasks,* (ASCD,1998). He also authored writing process textbooks for the Stack the Deck Writing Program, and he has published articles in *Educational Leadership, The Reading Teacher, Language Arts, Middle Ground,* and *Multimedia Schools.*

Index

Action research
    and effectiveness of teaching methods, 6
ACES
    academic performance clues and, 127, 130
    conduct clues and, 127–128
    and evaluating the effectiveness of instruction, 121
        illustrated chart of, 122, 136
    expressive clues and, 128–129
    outlined, 121
    sensing clues and, 129
    and teacher pedagogiofolio, 135

Brainy light bulb. *See also* the Open Mind
    as adaptation of the Open Mind, 13
        iluustrated, 13

Card games. *See also* ACES
    as a metaphor for teaching, xiii, 1, 7, 29, 30, 55, 79, 119, 121, 141
ChecBric, the. *See also* First Dare
    as a First Dare tool, 40–41
    and rubrics, 115
    as a scoring device, 40
        illustration of, 41
    as a student-friendly rubric, 116
Cibrowski, Jean. *See also* Repair on textbooks
    and student comprehension, 61–62

Click and clunk
    as a First Dare tool, 46
        examples of, outlined, 46
Collaborative Strategic Reading (CSR)
    CSR Learning Log, 14
        as adaptation of Preview tool, 14
        illustrated, 15
    Get the Gist originating from, 51
    and student cooperation, 14

Dabbs, Tracy. *See also* Share
    Monster Before and After visual tool invented by, 102–103
DeBono, Edward. *See also* Repair
    CoRT Thinking Program developed by, 65
    and OPV, 65–66
    and PMI, 68
Dimino, Joseph
    theory stops described by, 10

First Dare
    and the Checbric, 40
        illustrated, 41
    and click and clunk, 46
    and the Double-Column Entry, 33
        illustrated, 33
    and the Folded Bookmark, 47–48
    and the four-step template, 7–8, 122

outlined, 9
and graphic organizers, 48–50
and the My Reading—My Thinking Chart, 31–32
   illustration of, 32
and the Open Mind, 12
and the Open Turtle, 12–13
outline of, 30–31
and the Pocket Organizer, 46–47
   lower-performing students and, 47
and Prepare, 30–31
and SnapShots, 36–40
and sticky notes, 44–45
and storyboards, 40–43
   illustration of, 43
strategies of, outlined, 132–133
as a tool for processing new information, 5
types of questioning strategies for, 33–36
   examples of, 35

Focus questions
and the First Dare stage, 24
keywords for, 24–25
   examples of, 25
as a Prepare strategy, 24
and student reading, 26

Get the Gist. *See also* First Dare
as a First Dare tool, 51
Graphic organizers. *See also* First Dare
as First Dare tools, 48–50
   illustrations of, 49, 50
popularity of as a teaching tool, 48
similarity to the outline as a teaching tool, 48
software programs for, 48–50

Kaplan, Sandra
and focus questions, 24
on the role of questioning, 24
Klingner, Janette. *See also* Collaborative Strategic Research (CSR)
and codevelopment of click and clunk, 46
and codevelopment of Preview, 14
K-W-L
adaptations of, 21
   illustration of, 21
defined, 20
forecasting strategy as applied by students, 20
as a retrieving tool, 20

Langer, Judith
and higher student achievement, list of features present for, 51–52
and research on teaching and learning, 51

Lenz, K.
unit of study defined by, 18
Lewin, Larry
ChecBric developed by, 40
interviewed, 141–143
and key findings of teaching and learning research, as outlined by, 123–124
and the User Friendly Text Checklist, 62–63
   illustrated, 62–63

Marzano, Robert. *See also* William Sanders
teachers as a factor affecting student achievement, 10–11
Mental Floppy Disk. *See also* the Open Mind
as an adaptation of the Open Mind, 13–14
illustrated, 13

Ogle, Donna. *See also* K-W-L
K-W-L developed by, 20
Open Mind, the
adaptations of, 12–14
as an effective Prepare tool, 11–12
and First Dare stage
as a First Dare tool, 45
   illustrated, 45
illustrated, 11
Open Turtle, the
as adaptation of the Open Mind, 12
   illustrated, 12
as First Dare tool, 12–13

Personal Agenda, the. *See also* work plans
as an effective planning strategy for students, 21
sample illustration of, 22
Pocket organizer
as a First Dare strategy, 46–47
Prepare
and best practice teaching, 7–8
as first step in process approach, 7
and forecasting, 24
and the four-step template, 7–8, 122
   outlined, 9
and planning for instruction, 122–124
as a planning tool for teaching, 7
and Preview, 14
strategies for, outlined, 132
as a tool for preparing students, 5
tools and, 11–27
Preview
and CSR, 14
as modified by teachers, 14
as multimedia tool for teaching, 14, 15
and Microsoft PowerPoint®, 15
   presentation of, illustrated, 16

Index

features of, 15
as a Prepare tool, 14
process of, outlined, 14
as a student reading strategy, 14

QAR (Question Answer Relationship Strategy)
as a Prepare tool, 25–26
strategies of, outlined, 26
types of questions, outlined, 26

Repair
The Adapted Value Examination Matrix, 67–68
illustration of, 67
and analyzing perspectives, 67
and CCM (the Conceptual Change Model), 72
stages of, outlined, 72
and the challenge of addressing student misconceptions, 55–56
reasons for misconceptions, outlined, 61
and different types of knowledge, defined, 57–58
procedural knowledge, 58
declaritive knowledge, 59–60
conditional knowledge, 57
and First Dare stage, 57
and the four-step template, 7–8
outlined, 9
and the LINCS strategy, 68–69
as both a First Dare and Repair tool, 69
and Oodles of Noodles, 73
worksheet, illustrated, 74
and OPV, 65–66
and CoRT Thinking Program, 65
illustrated, 66
and PMI, 68
strategies of, outlined, 56, 133
and student comprehension, 5
and ThoughtShots, 69–70
and Umbrella Tella, 75–76
blackline of, illustrated, 75
as a Wild Card, 75
and the User Friendly Text Checklist, 62–63
illustrated, 62–63
and the Values Response Protocol, 64–65

Raphael, Taffy E. *See also* QAR
QAR created by, 26

Sanders, William. *See also* Robert Marzano
study on student achievement, 10–11
teachers as most effective factor on, 10–11

Share
and The Annotated Collection, 99–100
and student instruction, 99
versatility of, 100
and The Annotated Open Mind, 87–88
illustrated, 88
as assessment, 112–116
ChecBric used for, 115–116
formats for, 113–116
illustrated, 113–116
benefits of and importance of writing skills for, 82
and The Brochure, 88–91
and computer technology, 90
in language arts/literature classrooms, 89
popularity of in social studies classrooms, 88
samples of, 89, 90
and The Class Newspaper, 91–93
effectiveness of in teaching, 91
as a formal writing tool, 91
research, resources for, 92
sample of, 92
and comic books and comic strips, 104–106
effectiveness of as an integrated art lesson, 105
illustrated, 104, 107
as a modification of the SnapShots tool, 104
and EGOs (electronic graphic organizers), 107–108
effectiveness of with students, 107–108
sample, 108
software programs for, 107–108
and The Five-Minute Write, 85
and First Dare, 85
four modes of Sharing, listed, 82
and the four-step template, 7–8
and the I-Search, 100–102
example of, 101
as a research tool, 100
and The Letter, 85–87
examples of, 86, 87
and Monsters Before and After, 102–103
illustrations of, 103
and the Open Mind, 103
outlined, 9, 133–134
and Picture Book Critiques, 93–94
as a replacement for the book report, 93
and The Postcard, 83–85
illustrated, 83
Quick Writes as a writing tool, 82
and The Short Story, 96–98

    samples of, 96, 97
    student writing and, 96–98
    and The Simulated Trial, 109–110
        effectiveness of with students, 110
        and The Literature Play, 111–112
        and The Reader's Theatre, 110
    and Speaking, 108–109
        the power of dialogue and, 108
        Round Robin Minispeeches, 108–109
            and graphic organizers, 109
            illustrated, 106
    and The Story Diamond, 107
        illustrated, 107
    and technical writing, 94–96
        samples of, 94, 95
    as a tool for the sharing of knowledge, 5
Shoemaker, Betty
    ChecBric codeveloped by, 40
    interviewed, 141–143
    and the I-Search method, 100
    multimedia tool developed by, 15–16
    nd student feedback forms, 134–135
        sample, 134
    Tip of the Iceberg Wild Card developed by, 70
        illustrated, 70
    and the User Friendly Text Checklist, 62–63
        illustrated, 62–63
SnapShots. *See also* First Dare
    as a First Dare tool, 36–40
    and the Shakespearean Photo Album, 36–37, 39
        illustrated, 37
    and student visualization skills, 36, 38
Stephans, Joseph. *See also* Repair
    CCM developed by, 72
Storyboards
    defined, 40–41
    examples of, 42, 43
    as a First Dare tool, 40–43

Teachers
    challenge of student misconceptions as addressed by, 55–56
    development of student-friendly scoring guides, 130–134
        illustrations of, 130, 131
    and evaluation of instruction, 119–121
    as a factor in student achievement, 10–11
    and the four-step template, 8
    importance of data for, 136–139
    incorporating best practices, outlined, 125
    and pedagogiofolio, 126–127, 135, 136
        benefits of, listed, 126
    and performance-based assessment, 80–81
    and student values, 63–68
    and the tapping of students' conditional knowledge, 131
    teaching strategies for, listed, 5, 9
    and use of appropriate intervention, 76
    use of focus questions by to actively engage student knowledge, 24
    use of visuals by for instruction, 102
Teaching cards
    as method for teaching, 4
Tomlinson, Carol Ann. *See also* Personal Agenda
    agenda sample developed by, 21
        illustrated, 22
The Unit Organizer (Routine)
    and the four-step template, 18
    as a framework for the unit, 18
    illustrated, 19, 20
    as a method for organizing knowledge, 18
    as a powerful teaching and learning tool, 19–20
    as a Prepare tool, 18
    as a study guide for students, 19
    unit, defined, 18
    as a Wild Card, 18

Vaughn, Sharon. *See also* Collaborative Strategic Reading (CSR)
    and codevelopment of click and clunk, 46
    and codevelopment of Preview, 14

Weill, Paul. *See also* Repair
    Oodles of Noodles Repair tool developed by, 73
        illustrations of, 74
Wild Cards
    Tip of the Iceberg as, 70
    Umbrella Tella as, 75
    Unit Organizer Routine labeled as, 18
    versatility of as teaching tools, 6
Work plans
    calendars as, 23
        illustrated, 23
    and the Personal Agenda, 21
        illustrated, 22
    and student book reports, 22–23
        sample work plan for, 22
    as term preferred for agendas, 22